COUPLES
IN LOVE

COUPLES IN LOVE

Straight Talk on Dating, Respect, Commitment, Marriage, and Sexuality

John R. Waiss

A Crossroad Book
The Crossroad Publishing Company
New York

The Crossroad Publishing Company
481 Eighth Avenue, New York, NY 10001

Printed in the United States of America

Library of Congress Cataloging-in-Publication Data

Waiss, John R., 1957-
    Couples in love : straight talk on dating, respect, commitment, marriage, and sexuality / John R. Waiss.
       p. cm.
    Includes bibliographical references.
    ISBN 0-8245-2130-7 (alk. paper)
    1. Sex–Religious aspects–Catholic Church. 2. Love–Religious aspects–Catholic Church. 3. Marriage–Religious aspects–Catholic Church. 4. Catholic Church–Doctrines. I. Title.
BX1795.S48W35 2003
241'.66–dc21

                        2003012924

1 2 3 4 5 6 7 8 9 10   08 07 06 05 04 03

To the Mother of Pure Love,
May I only have eyes for you!

Contents

Foreword

Too often Catholic Church teaching on sexual ethics is thought to consist of a long litany of "No, No, No!" and "Thou shalt not," expressing a fundamentally negative approach to human sexuality. On the contrary, Church teaching rests on a very positive view of the body and sexuality, grounded in the primacy of self-giving love.

Father John Waiss has done extensive work with young people who are dating, with couples preparing for marriage, as well as with young married couples. This volume is the fruit of his many years of conversations with young couples. He has had to answer thorny questions about the Church's position on human sexuality, questions often asked of priests and others involved in the ministry of marriage preparation. Father Waiss's straightforward articulation of Church teaching in a clear and convincing manner is refreshing. But what is truly unique about this volume is the way in which the author lays out the Christian ideal within the framework of an ongoing conversation between a priest, "Father JP," and a young couple: "Sam," a nonpracticing Jew and "Margie," a young Catholic woman who has recently returned to active participation in the Church. The dialogue between Father JP and the young couple provides the context for a volley of questions and answers, throwing light on the many issues encountered by young people who are serious about their faith, and who recognize that the body and sexuality are gifts to be treasured rather than objects to be used and squandered.

The insights gleaned from these pages run against the grain of a culture such as ours that all too often depersonalizes and dehumanizes sexuality. Father Waiss's contribution lies in a view of human sexuality consistent with the "logic of love" rooted in the self-gift of Christ, giving rise to an understanding of sexual expression as mutual self-gift within an enduring relationship of profound respect and care for one another.

Whether it is used for personal enrichment, classroom use, discussion groups, or as a conversation starter for those who work with young couples, *Couples in Love* will prove to be a helpful tool for coming to a deeper appreciation not only of Church teaching, but also of the reasons why the Church teaches what it does. Eminently practical without watering down the truth about the responsibilities that are ours because of the gift of sexuality, Father JP's responses to the hard questions raised by Margie and, especially, Sam, are reflective of a long and strong tradition that cherishes and safeguards sexuality as a gift of love through which we share in the divine life.

His Eminence
Cardinal Roger Mahony
Archbishop of Los Angeles

The Exciting *Gospel of Love and Life*

The Challenge

Judeo-Christian morality, especially sexual morality, has been under brutal attack for years. Often portrayed as a set of old-fashioned taboos and negative precepts from Jewish Scriptures — that is, the Old Testament — "modern" society finds no objective foundation or utility in it.

Our education system reduces sexuality to a biological urge. The media depicts it as an ordinary, commonplace, and meaningless activity on par with daily sports, news, and weather. But people hunger for love, especially the youth.

Radical individualism and moral subjectivism permeates our culture. They exalt an exercise of freedom independent of others, so that an individual can and should be able to do anything as long as it doesn't hurt anybody. Applied to sexual ethics, this means "two mutually consenting adults can do anything they want as long as it don't hurt anybody else."

Moreover, many parents, teachers, and pastors of souls fail to proclaim the Christian view of human love and sexuality. Some seem ashamed, while others seem not to know how. Perhaps they fear losing young people by demanding what seems impossible to live, or fear appearing inadequately foolish in responding to the skeptical questioning of a rebellious teen. Perhaps it is just easier to "go with the flow," even if it means "selling out" to the overwhelming "culture of death" and promiscuity.

The Opportunity

With material prosperity, few see the need for religion or prayer. "I don't need God. I have all that I could possibly want. I am in control of my life" or so goes the thinking. But this way of thinking leads to life without meaning, including a superficial and empty sexuality based on biological urges without commitment or love. Love itself loses its meaning.

But people — especially young people — long for love; they long to love and be loved with true depth. They search for a vision of sex full of lasting meaning, but few find it.

This is a fantastic opportunity for the Gospel. The Church's teaching on love and human sexuality may be one of the few paths back to faith and God. It is not just a portion of the Gospel, but an essential compendium and "sacrament" of the "good news": the Gospel of Life and Love.

The Hope

The Christian personalism of Pope John Paul II offers us much hope. In analyzing morality, traditional Judeo-Christian ethics has focused on obedience to authority and law, whether natural or positive law. Without rejecting this or abandoning it as unimportant, personalism teaches us to value what an action *says,* that is, to value the *objective* and *intrinsic meaning* each action conveys.

Personalism affirms that our actions — when fulfilling the law — are statements that enrich and deepen relationships, or — when breaking the law — statements that denigrate and tarnish those relationships. Herein lies its power to address modernity. Instead of asking "Does this action violate some law?" we ask, "What does this action *say* and how does it affect my relationship to those I love?" For example, a mother may punish her two sons for breaking the family rule against fighting (traditional ethics). Or, she may address each son individually regarding how his fighting affects her personally, that her love for each of them is so deep that when one strikes the other it is as if he were striking her (personalist approach).

The question of Sunday Mass for Catholics is another example. Not wanting to attend Mass, many young people invent convincing arguments why they need not go. Perhaps they say, "I can pray and worship God at home. The results are the same. Besides, I'm not hurting anybody by not going." Their parents often argue from authority: "We must attend Mass because the Church says so. Not to go would violate God's commandment." In this exchange, neither parents nor child wins, and God comes out appearing like a tyrant.

Yet the personalist would ask, "What do I say by missing Sunday Mass, and, how does that affect my relationship with God?" The reasoning becomes clear, especially when contrasted with a human relationship. For example, how would a girl react to her boyfriend saying, "Sweetheart, I am glad that you're my girl. You love me a lot and I love you a lot. We have this special bond between us. But let's face it, you're a busy girl, with all your sports and extracurricular activity, and I'm a busy guy. Let's just plan on seeing each other once a month or so. What do you say?"

Any girl with a bit of sense would be greatly upset, because this boy's action was telling her (what it really said is) that he didn't really love her. She would probably reply angrily, "Look, I'll find someone else, thank you, someone who will make time for me!" Would anyone like to hear God saying that to him: "I'll find someone else, someone who will make time for me"? Deliberately missing Sunday Mass *says* we really do not love Jesus Christ, who is there for us but we are not there for Him.

The Approach

Christian personalism approaches sexuality as inherently good. In this somewhat new approach, I am guided and motivated by Saint Josemaría Escrivá, the founder of Opus Dei, who blessed the marriage bed with both hands, boldly proclaiming the *joyful affirmation*[1] of chastity. His first successor, Bishop Alvaro del Portillo, powerfully summed up his teaching:

15

There is nothing more diametrically opposed to the teaching of the Church than contempt or belittlement of material realities. Therefore, Christian doctrine affirms without hesitation that in the Incarnation of the Word, everything that is proper to man, body and soul, spirit and matter, has been assumed and elevated to an undreamed of dignity in Jesus Christ. . . . The Holy Trinity wants us to have the holy pride of practicing the virtue of purity. . . . A clean and chaste life, enlivened by charity, directs the whole human person to God, even our corporeality, to the fullness of love and happiness.[2]

In contrast, Manichaeanism views sexuality and the body as evil. This view infected early Christian thought with different and recurring forms of Puritanism. Augustine and later Aquinas tried to recover a positive character of human sexuality as created by God, nevertheless, they never quite overcame the negativity associated with concupiscence and passion — the *psychological-emotional dimension* of sexuality — as the principal source of sexual sins.[3] Yet there is no inherent reason to condemn this dimension which God created good.

The *psychological-emotional* dimension of sexuality deeply influences a person's life, for good or bad. But in affirming its intrinsic goodness, personalism develops an integral vision of the person and sexuality: personalism unites the knowledge of the biology and health aspects (emphasized in sex-education classes) with the *psychological-emotional* and the *moral-religious* dimensions, integrating them into a single outlook. This integration of sexuality into the whole person, while respecting the intimacy and sacredness of sexual love, makes a virtuous life easier and more attractive.[4] The *Catechism of the Catholic Church* says it well:

Chastity means the successful integration of sexuality within the person and thus the inner unity of man in his bodily and spiritual being. Sexuality, in which man's belonging to the bodily and biological world is expressed, becomes personal and truly human when it is integrated

*into the relationship of one person to another, in the
complete and lifelong mutual gift of a man and a woman.*

*The virtue of chastity therefore involves the integrity of
the person and the integrality of the gift.* (CCC 2337)

The Book

I have found the Socratic-like dialogue the most natural way to
discuss the issues of love, dating, and sexuality, since most of
the questions addressed arose in individual or in small group
discussions.

I have made the dialogue as natural as possible. In real
face-to-face situations, one can easily repeat ideas, give further
examples, and explore other creative explanations to clarify a
point misunderstood, especially when confronted with the be-
wildered face of a listener. In a book, such repetition becomes
tedious and it is impossible to anticipate every confusion and
misapprehension of such a broad readership.

I try to keep this work short and accessible. This is not an ex-
haustive theological or philosophical treatise, nor is it possible
to address every question. Some arguments may not be convincing. My goal is to make young people think, giving them
sufficient rationale to convince most that answers to their questions do exist, although they may have to invest some effort
themselves to seek them out.

The Reader

This work is directed to conscientious young people who are
willing to question and challenge current modes of behavior, to
those who think and care about doing what is right, and to those
who search for true and long-term happiness for themselves and
others.

I expect engaged couples — and those nearing that stage in
their relationship — to benefit from this book in preparing for
marriage and their life together. Parents — the primary teachers
of their children — pastors, priests, teachers, and other youth

leaders should find it useful as a complement to their own explanations and experience. Whether you employ this for your own reading and personal enrichment, or in the classroom and discussion groups, I hope you will find it an effective instrument for understanding and explaining the truths about sexual morality and the value of chastity.

The Setting
of the Dialogue

Sam is a twenty-six-year-old bachelor. Although his father was a nonpracticing Christian, Sam's Jewish mother considered religion to be an essential part of his upbringing. Sam made his bar mitzvah when he was thirteen but, like many of his peers, has done very little since to practice his Jewish faith. He had a promiscuous past and sees nothing wrong with sex before marriage.

Meeting Margie created a personal conflict for Sam. He saw something very special in her from their first encounter, although he wasn't sure what it was. The two had been seeing each other for several months. In this short period of time, Sam fell deeply in love with her — more than with any woman he had ever met. He did not want to lose her, but it bothered him that she refused to sleep with him.

Margie is twenty-three and single. She was raised a Catholic, although she too left her faith behind when she went away to college. Like Sam, she also went too far in previous relationships and now regrets it. Recently she rediscovered Christ and returned to her faith. She now regularly goes to confession and Sunday Mass. Part of her efforts to change and lead a better life motivated her to volunteer at a program to assist disabled children. This is where she and Sam met, both as volunteers. Margie is very attracted to Sam's human virtues, manly character, and tender heart — especially in dealing with these children — although she resents his sexual advances. Despite her past mistakes, Margie still considers herself a virgin, which is important to her.

Since they are lovingly devoted to each other, Sam does not see why Margie is unwilling to be sexually intimate with him, especially since she has had previous sexual experiences. Sam realizes that her return to practicing her faith has caused her to become less physical in her affection toward him.

Margie knows her faith does not allow a person to have sex before marriage, but she is at a loss to explain why. Sam, on the other hand, is quite good at coming up with many reasonable arguments — "sex is such a beautiful thing" and "it is perfectly OK for two people who really love each other." In fact, he runs circles around Margie on this point, with convincing answers to all her objections. Yet Margie refuses to budge.

Finally Sam gets an idea. "Let's go to your minister and talk to him about this," he suggests to Margie. "If he can come up with reasonable arguments as to why sex is bad for us, I will respect your wishes." He thinks that if he can show how outdated and negative the Christian view of sexuality is in front of an authority that Margie respects, perhaps she might then let go of her inhibitions and allow their love to develop more openly and physically. Not knowing his full intentions, Margie agrees to Sam's idea, thinking that this might be the opportunity for him to understand and appreciate her beliefs in this matter.

The two make an appointment with a young parish priest, who is fondly known as Father "JP" by the young people he helps. Father JP is also very much involved in preparing couples for marriage, a role that he truly enjoys.

Father JP is a man of his era, growing up in the same oversexed culture as Sam and Margie. He, too, experienced the overt and objectified way sex is presented in sex education classes in high school and was exposed to television programs where sex is treated as a casual activity. While growing up, he had deep personal conversations with friends who would share with him their joys and disappointments, their problems and worries, and sometimes even their sexual exploits. A great concern for his friends led Father JP to think and pray in order to find ways to help them. He tends to be direct, because he wrestles with their struggles and search for meaning. And as a firm believer, Father JP is impassioned about finding ways to teach that Faith in a more convincing manner, especially ways that speak to the minds and hearts of young people.

After introducing themselves to each other, Father JP suggests that Sam simply call him "JP," since Sam is not Catholic and, therefore, does not consider Father JP as a spiritual father to him. Sam appreciates that, because he would indeed have felt odd calling JP "Father."

Is Christian Morality Negative?

After their introductions, Sam begins questioning Father JP.

Should Celibate Priests Tell Couples What to Do with Their Bodies?

Sam: JP, I hope you don't mind if I am frank with you.

Father JP: Don't worry, Sam, I can take it. I'd rather you be frank than mask your real thoughts and concerns.

Sam: OK. My main problem with the Catholic teaching on sexuality is that it is not realistic. It expects normal people to behave like robots with no emotions. That's because those setting Church policy are celibate men. They have little or no experience with sexuality and love and they repress their natural feelings. What is an unmarried celibate man, who doesn't even date, doing telling married and dating couples what to do with their bodies? It's like a bus driver telling a surgeon how to do open heart surgery.

Father JP: First, Sam, Catholic teaching on sexuality doesn't depend on celibate priests alone. Our beliefs come from God and originate in the teaching of the Hebrew Scriptures. It was those Jewish priests — who happened to be married, by the way — who handed those teachings down to us.

Second, priests do have a lot more experience than you think. In hearing confessions and giving spiritual direction, they deal with moral dilemmas from all sorts of people: from the five- and six-year-olds to people in their seventies and eighties; male

Bless me, Father, for I have sinned . . .

and female; married and dating; single mothers and fathers, and those living in all kinds of sinful or saintly situations. Priests experience quite a bit in a very short period of time, like a doctor in a residency program. Seminary training helps priests give consistent advice in these very diverse cases.

Just because a priest hasn't experienced something firsthand doesn't mean he can't give good advice. Does a doctor have to go through cancer and its treatment to identify and cure it? Does one have to have abused children or do drugs to be able to tell someone else that it is wrong? Do teachers have to visit Japan, India, or Nigeria to be able to teach their students about the history, geography, and culture of these countries?

Sam: No, of course not.

Father JP: Then why must we say that a priest has to be dating or married to give advice to those who are dating or married? Many good coaches of college and professional sports never played the sport competitively.

Besides, celibate priests are not emotionless robots. We deal with the same emotions that you do. We feel the same attraction to beautiful women, and we, too, struggle to keep these emotions from controlling the decisions we make and the life we live. This gives us a certain freedom to integrate — with God's help — that dimension of our lives into our vocation to love God and others.

Priests are called to love the people whom we are called to serve with a father's heart. We try to be understanding of their frailties while encouraging and challenging them in their struggles.

Why Is Judeo-Christian Morality So Negative?

Sam: But JP, you must admit that Christian morality seems awfully negative and strict: *You shall not kill. You shall not commit adultery. You shall not steal, cheat, or lie.* Wouldn't it be easier to say *You shall have no fun?* And when it comes to something so positive, so intensely enriching and fulfilling as expressing one's love in sex, Christian morality is full of old-fashioned, negative hang-ups:

- *No sex before marriage.*
- *No extramarital affairs.*
- *No passionate caressing and kissing outside of marriage.*
- *No contraception, even within marriage.*
- *Even, no thoughts and desires for sex!*

I don't mean to offend you, JP, but it seems as though "moral" people like yourself just don't know how to enjoy something good like sex. You seem to treat it as if it were something dirty or evil — something you want to hide or keep in the closet. Why?

Father JP: Sam, you're right! If Christian morality were just a collection of negative precepts, then it would be empty. I would be the first to join you and the masses in rejecting this teaching and embrace the so-called "free love."

Sam: You would?

24

Father JP: I said I would *if* Christian morality were just a collection of negative precepts. However, I have found it to be much more than that. In fact, the more I talk to people like you who challenge me to think and to delve into the notion and meaning of true love, the more I discover the wisdom and consistency of what has been taught and lived for thousands of years. It was just a few years ago that our society decided to jettison the wisdom of years of experience. What is considered Christian moral teaching was Jewish moral teaching thousands of years prior to Christ. The Jews claimed to have received it from God, but it is more than just a claim because in it there is clearly something special, something "divine." The wisdom of Christian and Jewish moral teaching can be seen as both true and beautiful, even by non-Christians and non-Jews.

But, Sam and Margie, do you really think you are ready to discover the truth and the beauty of pure love? Are you up to the task?

Margie: Yes, I am.

Father JP: And you, Sam?

Sam: I'm ready to discuss this, but I want you to know that I'm not a pushover. I won't accept platitudes or rules for rules' sake, or some kind of partial or theoretical truth about love.

Father JP: You know, we are not talking about just some theoretical truth. This teaching on love requires action; it entails a call to live it. If you see the truth in it — in fact, in order to be open to see the truth in it — you must be ready to try to live it.

Sam: Yes, I'm aware of that. I wasn't born yesterday! But on the other hand, if it is not true, then living a so-called "moral" life is foolish, one of the most foolish things in the world. Something that I hope Margie will realize. Margie, are you ready for this?

Margie: Well, I've made some mistakes in the past. I feel I've lost part of my innocence, which I would really like to recover. I don't know if that is possible, but certainly I want to make sure that I do not lose any more of it. That's why we're here.

Father JP: Well, I admire your forthrightness and willingness to discuss these things. I pray that each one of us will have the strength of character not only to hear each other out, but also to live out the consequences of the truth we discover.

Negative Precepts Reflect Positive Values

Sam: Getting back to my question, then, why is Christian morality so negative?

Father JP: Let's take a look at the Ten Commandments. Are they really so negative? Can we not glean some positive teaching or value from them?

For example, doesn't the commandment, "You shall not kill," tell us something positive?

Margie: Sure it does — it tells us that life is precious.

Father JP: Exactly! Human life is precious. In fact, it's not only precious — it's sacred! By this commandment, God tells us that the dignity of each person is so great that he will severely punish us if we disregard its sacredness.

You could look at it another way. Often we hear reports that a certain behavior is unhealthy, for example, that regular smoking will decrease your life expectancy by X number of years. These reports usually conclude by condemning the unhealthy behavior: "Don't smoke; it'll kill you."

If someone were to do a controlled study on the life expectancy of murderers and just happen to discover that murderers — on the average — lived 18.7 years less than the population as a whole, perhaps that report would conclude, "Don't kill others because it'll kill you." Perhaps such a report would have little effect on die-hard murderers. However, it might motivate someone to think twice before following through with shooting another human being.

Sam: It's hard for me to imagine people thinking about how long they're going to live while they're planning to murder someone.

*Headlines: Murderers Have Reduced Life-Expectancy
of 18.7 Years*

Father JP: You're probably right. However, if we consider our eternal life expectancy, how a particular action may affect our lot after death, then the fear of losing heaven and suffering eternally may motivate a few more individuals.

Sam: That's if you believe in God, heaven, and hell.

Father JP: True. You can argue that if God does not exist, then nothing would be immoral; one could do anything he wanted — steal, murder, abuse women or children — with no fear of eternal retribution. The point I was trying to make is negative precepts do reflect positive values. "You shall not kill" reflects the sacredness of life while warning us of potential negative consequences by choosing to ignore that sacredness.

Sam: I'm not saying that it's OK to murder or abuse children. Those things are wrong. But let's be real. It's easy to show how murder harms the person killed, his family, and society in general. Sex between consenting adults doesn't hurt anyone. Sex is not bad or dirty. It's good — very good. So why does the Catholic Church look down on it?

Father JP: Sam, let me ask you this: would you say that it doesn't matter if the woman you marry has had sex with another man?

Sam: Well, it would be nice if I was the first one in her life, but I wouldn't hold her to a higher standard than I would myself. So it wouldn't bother me if she had.

Father JP: What if her previous sex partner was one of your best friends?

Sam: That might be a little different, but I think I could handle that.

Father JP: How about when you are married and your friend comes over to visit? You don't think it would affect how you viewed your friend or how he viewed you? You don't think it would affect the way your friend and your wife interact?

Sam: Well, you're right, it might put a damper on the friendship a bit.

Father JP: Taking this a step further, what if the person your wife had sex with was your brother or even your father? Or what if this man had genital herpes, or HIV, or some venereal disease? Would any of this matter?

Sam: Well, yes. I don't think I'd marry her under those conditions.

If only you were Charlie...

Father JP: Let's suppose your wife-to-be didn't fall under any of those conditions. However, she occasionally experienced uncontrollable flashbacks of sexual engagements that she had with previous partners. This occurred especially when she was sexually aroused. Would that affect your decision to marry her?

Sam: That would be difficult to deal with. Making love with a woman I knew was thinking about someone else would be kind of repulsive.

Father JP: You seem to be saying, then, that a woman or man who is not a virgin — at least under certain circumstances —

is damaged goods, and that somehow she or he has been victimized by her past sexual experiences.

Sam: But these are extreme examples.

Father JP: Perhaps, but they do occur and much more frequently than you think. Moreover, perhaps less extreme sexual experiences inflict lesser damage, but they still cause damage.

How Lust Affects Love

Impure Glances

Sam: JP, that's hard to prove. It seems that you're putting up a smoke screen to cover up the negativity of Christian morality.

For example, one taboo that exemplifies the negativity of Christian morality is the commandment against certain glances and looks. People have told me that Christians consider lustful looks and thoughts sinful, even "mortally" sinful! That's ludicrous. How can looking at another person be a sin? If I am not hurting anyone, what wrong am I doing? Are you saying that the beauty of the human body is so bad that looking at it is sinful?

Father JP: Sam, the Judeo-Christian tradition has always considered the human body as a beautiful masterpiece of God's creation. It is something good. However, one can distort and abuse something good by using it as an object of one's own selfish pleasure.

Let's try to put the question of lust in the context of a human relationship. This example may help. Let's imagine a young couple in love. In fact, we can imagine you and Margie walking down the street together holding hands, conversing, having a great time together.

Margie: We do that all the time. Just being together is something special.

Father JP: Now imagine that as the two of you walk down the street together you happen upon an immodestly dressed woman. Now this scene is fictitious. I am not saying that this is what you would do, but let's suppose, Sam, thinking that it

Ugh...I thought you loved me.

means nothing, you take a glance at the immodestly dressed woman. Then you start admiring her, turning your head and following her with your eyes — and bang! You run into a telephone pole!

Now, Sam, how do you think Margie would react? What would she think?

Sam: She might laugh or think, "Ah, he deserves it."

Margie: Laugh? No way! I'd be livid!

Father JP: Now remember, we're just imagining. Nevertheless, there is no denying that Margie would be hurt and rightfully so. She could be so hurt that she would walk out on you right then and there.

Sam: Aren't you going a bit far? Is it really such a big deal?

Margie: Oh yes, it is! Sam, it would mean that you...well it would be as if...

Father JP: It would be as if you had been unfaithful to Margie, unfaithful with your eyes. We could consider it a "mortal" sin against her, because it would or could kill your relationship with her.

Sam: But wait a minute, JP. I still think you're going too far when you say that any glance at a beautiful woman is seriously sinful. Yes, I see how looking at another woman could hurt Margie, and I would never knowingly hurt her. The important thing seems to be to avoid hurting the person you love. I don't see anything wrong with "feasting" my eyes on a woman's beauty, as long as it doesn't hurt anyone. Why else would God make the woman's body so beautiful?

Father JP: Sam, there is nothing essentially wrong for a married man to "feast" his eyes on his wife's bodily beauty. It is part of his love and may even enhance his love for her. Nor is it wrong to appreciate the bodily beauty of women in general. That is why the Catholic Church sees nothing inherently wrong with nudity in art. When nudity in art avoids the erotic — that is, avoids directly stimulating the sexual appetites — it can be something good because it helps us to appreciate the beauty of God's creation and how God made woman for man and man for woman.

For example, if the two of you were visiting a museum together and you were to stop and admire an ancient Roman statue of a nude woman, how would you react, Margie?

Margie: I don't think it would bother me at all. I just can't see getting hurt over a statue — unless Sam started really "feasting" his eyes on the statue to the point of lusting over it. But it wouldn't offend me as much as disgust me.

Sam: Margie, that would be sick. I'd never do that.

Margie: I hope not.

Wow, you bet I love art!

Father JP: What is important here is what we *say* by our action. The reason why looking at a statue doesn't affect your relationship is because the statue is not directed toward any particular person. Do you know any woman who would think that her boyfriend was being unfaithful to her with his eyes by admiring the beauty of women reflected in a statue? Do you think that she would feel that now she was competing with a statue for her boyfriend's love and attention?

Margie: No, of course not, that would be ridiculous.

Father JP: So, Sam, we agree that nudity in art is not in itself immoral.

In what other occasion would you find "feasting" your eyes on another woman not hurtful to Margie and your relationship with her?

Sam: Well, if I were just hanging out with the guys admiring pretty women, as long as Margie wasn't there. You know — doing the typical male thing of admiring beautiful women. It wouldn't be directed against Margie.

Margie: (*with surprise and almost anger in her voice*) Do you think it would be OK just because I wasn't there?

Sam: Oh, Margie, I didn't mean it that way. I was just proposing a hypothetical example for the discussion.

Father JP: Margie, have patience with Sam and me. We men often propose "theoretical" arguments without realizing how severely it could affect our relationships. That is why I like discussing these matters with you and Sam together, because that makes him think twice about "theoretical" attitudes that actually affect your relationship.

Margie: OK, Father JP, I'm sorry. I guess I'm a little sensitive about these matters.

Father JP: No, you are not too sensitive at all, Margie. As I said, I think it helps us have a more honest discussion.

Let's go on. Sam, let me propose another hypothetical example for you: What if you and your buddies were to go to a topless bar without Margie knowing it? Do you think it would not affect her and your relationship with her just because she wasn't present? And what if she were later to find out, perhaps because she just happened to see you walking out or one of your buddies ended up telling her. Would that not hurt her and your relationship with her?

Sam: You're right there, but that is extreme and raunchy behavior.

Father JP: It is true that I may use more extreme examples to illustrate the principles. Don't you think it makes a difference to

Margie how you behave even though she isn't present? Do we need other examples to prove the point?

Sam: OK, you're right. It does make a difference, though I wouldn't think that it could do that much damage. But now that you mention it, it does kind of make sense.

Margie: Father JP, you said that it is OK for a husband to "feast" his eyes on his wife. But isn't that also lust?

Father JP: That's a very good point, Margie, one that many people miss. If a man looks at his wife as a mere object of sexual satisfaction, then it would be sinful lust. In such a case, it doesn't matter whether the woman is his wife or not, because it disregards her dignity as a human person.

However, if he looks at his wife's beauty in a way that draws him to appreciate her free and complete gift of herself to him, and if it draws him to give himself more generously and unconditionally to her, that is, even without the condition of the sexual union, then such a bodily attraction can be something good, conducive to a happier marriage, because it respects her dignity as a person and leads to a more complete self-giving.

In the book of Tobit, the angel Raphael warned Tobias:

Hear me, and I will show you who are those over whom the devil can prevail. For they who enter into matrimony in such a manner as to shut out God from themselves and from their mind, and to give themselves to their lust, as the horse and the mule which have not understanding, are those over whom the devil has power. (Tobit 6:16–17, Septuagint)

Of course, this kind of lust is not limited to men. The same could be said of a woman "feasting" her eyes on her husband.

Sam: But, JP, do you really think your God cares about all this? Doesn't He have more important things to deal with in the world?

Father JP: Sam, this is the *logic of love*. God truly loves each one of us much more than any woman could love a man. The

36

Jewish Scripture says that He is a jealous God (Deuteronomy 4:24) worthy of all our love. What do we say to God when we look at a woman with lust in our heart? Are we not saying to Him, "Guess what, Lord, you have competition and you happen to be losing that competition right now." How do you think it would affect our relationship to Him?

Sam: I guess He wouldn't like it.

Father JP: That's quite an understatement. To guard one's eyes and one's heart is an expression of love, not a fear of tainting oneself with something dirty. This is why Jesus stated the matter so forcefully to His followers:

> *You have heard that it was said, 'You shall not commit adultery.' But I say to you that every one who looks at a woman lustfully has already committed adultery with her in his heart. If your right eye causes you to sin, pluck it out and throw it away; it is better that you lose one of your members than that your whole body be thrown into hell. And if your right hand causes you to sin, cut it off and throw it away; it is better that you lose one of your members than that your whole body go into hell.* (Matthew 5:27–30)

Jesus is explaining in a clear and graphic manner what God had already laid down in the Ten Commandments given to Moses:

> *You shall not covet . . . your neighbor's wife, or his manservant, or his maidservant.* (Exodus 20:17, cf. Deuteronomy 5:21)

The Psalms also convey this beautiful message where God says:

> *I will walk with integrity of heart within my house; I will not set before my eyes anything that is base. . . . The man of haughty looks and arrogant heart I will not endure.* (Psalm 101:2–5)

Sirach warns of the danger of lust:

Do not look intently at a virgin, lest you stumble and incur penalties for her.... Turn away your eyes from a shapely woman, and do not look intently at beauty belonging to another; many have been misled by a woman's beauty, and by it passion is kindled like a fire. (Sirach 9:5, 8)

In another place, the Psalmist asks God to help him preserve his love for God:

Turn my eyes from looking at vanities..... My eyes are awake before the watches of the night, that I may meditate upon your promise. (Psalm 119:37, 148)

For people in love, every action impacts their relationship, even short glances. The struggle to acquire self-control over one's eyes and over one's thoughts is a great manifestation of someone who truly wants to love another person and to show his or her love for God completely. Anything less is not love.

Saying "I Love You" with Your Eyes

Sam: That's all fine and good, but, JP, it's still fairly negative. The constant preoccupation with not offending God or the person one loves seems just too obsessive.

Father JP: True, but we haven't finished the argument yet. Let's recast our example in a positive light. Go back to the scene and imagine you and Margie — that young couple in love — walking down the street together. Again, you're holding hands and conversing, having a great time. Now as you walk together, again you happen upon that immodestly dressed woman. This time, however, you don't look. Imagine, Sam, you just continue walking as though you didn't even notice the other woman. Perhaps you turn instead and look into Margie's eyes.

How would she react? Do you think Margie would notice?

Margie: You bet I'd notice. It would be as if Sam said, "Wow, you are really special!"

38

Wow! How his eyes love me!

Father JP: Yes, indeed. It would be as if he were saying, "Margie, I only have eyes for you. I only have a heart for you." By not looking, Sam, you can *say* a lot. In fact, that not looking *says* more than repeating, "I love you, dear," hundreds of times. It means so much more.

Now if God really loves each one of us more than any woman could love a man, then our struggle *not* to look at impure sights, or our struggle to avoid impure imaginings and fantasies is seen by God as a *positive* act of love. This is why we can say with the Jewish Psalmist, "My eyes are ever toward the Lord" (Psalm 25:15).

Sam: Margie, I can't say whether God exists or not. Even if He were to exist, I don't know how much He would care about my thoughts and imaginings. But I want you to know that if I have ever slipped up here and offended you — and I am sure I have — I want you to know that I am sorry. Please don't hold it against me.

Margie: Of course I forgive you. Do you forgive me for any time I may have offended you unknowingly?

Sam: (*half jokingly, half seriously*) I do this time but remember, even God gets jealous!

Christians Should Not Be Afraid of Temptations

Father JP: Yes, this is what the logic of love is about: controlling or failing to control our eyes and thoughts does indeed affect our love.

Sam: I think I get your point. Still, it's neurotic to worry all the time about what we see and what we think. Let's face it, temptations are part of life.

Father JP: That's right. Yet, true Christians are not neurotic people because we don't fear temptations. In fact, we can even look forward to them. Temptations are opportunities to say, "I love you" to God and to the people we truly love. As long as we ignore temptations and move on, as long as we do not entertain the temptations but turn toward the person we love, then we avoid sin and make a great affirmation of love.

Sam: You say we should look *forward* to temptations? That sounds sick.

Father JP: We shouldn't deliberately put ourselves in situations that could lead us to sin, but when such situations arise without our looking for them, then we can seize the opportunity to manifest our love to God and to the person we love.

In other words, you would not take Margie into a topless bar just to show her that you won't look. However, when you encounter an immodestly dressed woman, you can take advantage of the opportunity to show your love for her in a way that means much more than any external act of affection. You can look forward to that!

Margie: But, Father, sometimes I feel like I sin in my thoughts, even though I think I've rejected them. I don't feel like I'm loving Our Lord. And what if I have thoughts for Sam?

Father JP: I could answer that question now, but we've covered a lot already. Besides, some things, which belong to the intimacy of our conscience, are better dealt with one-on-one when we go to confession. Margie, after your next confession — if you want to — just ask to talk about this topic in more detail. Then I will give you some advice to help you improve your personal relationship with God and your relationship with Sam in this regard.

Margie: OK, Father, I'll do that.

Father JP: Sam, maybe you, too, would like to come in sometime to chat one-on-one without Margie, to deal with some more personal topics, things having to do with you and God.

Sam: JP, I don't know about that. I came here to deal with my relationship with Margie. My relationship or my lack of relationship with God is a different matter.

Father JP: I'll respect that. I just want you to know that I am available. I hope this conversation has given you some things to think about.

Margie: Yes, Father, it has. Thank you.

Sam: It has, but I still have other questions for you.

Father JP: Great! We will tackle them next time.

Handling Temptations

A few days after Sam and Margie met with Father JP, Margie went to confession to him. Certain thoughts, dreams, and sensations bothered, almost tormented, her because it was difficult to discern what was sinful and what was not. So, after confession, Margie took advantage of her visit to the confessional to get some advice from Father JP concerning these struggles.

Are All Impure Thoughts Sins?

Margie: Father, this is Margie. Thank you for hearing my confession. I feel so relieved to know that Christ has forgiven all my sins. It fills me with joy and peace.

The other day you suggested that I bring up the subject of whether I sin each time I have an impure thought, dream, or sensation. Can you help me on this?

Father JP: Of course. First, don't be surprised. This struggle is quite common. In fact, everybody struggles with this to some degree. It is part of the tension between our spiritual and material sides. Temptations shouldn't bother us as long as we try to take advantage of them to show our love, as we discussed earlier.

Margie: Thank you for talking with us. It was a real eye-opener for me as well as for Sam.

Father JP: Well, your Sam is quite a guy. He has many great qualities and virtues. It takes quite some courage to talk about a topic like this with a priest, especially, since he is not even Catholic.

Margie: Yes, he is special. That is why I question whether having thoughts and desires for him are sinful.

Father JP: Try keeping your relationship with Sam pure and holy, even in your thoughts. As you consider which direction this relationship will lead, thoughts and desires for him will naturally arise. They may even arouse some sensuality but that is when you should react. Don't let selfishness exploit those thoughts and desires for pleasure and fantasy. That would turn Sam into an object and complicate your motives for being with him, making it more difficult for you to distinguish between true love and infatuation, or even lust. Do you remember that example I gave the two of you about walking down the street and encountering the immodestly dressed woman?

Margie: How could I forget it?

Father JP: You might want to turn that into a kind of prayer.

Margie: How so?

Father JP: Well, try repeating a short, little aspiration such as, "Jesus, may I only have eyes for you. May I only have a heart for you." If you go about repeating this as a kind of prayerful background music, then when a temptation comes up — perhaps a fantasy about Sam — this prayer will come to mind. It will trigger you to think about what you are *saying* to Jesus by allowing that fantasy to continue.

Margie: That sounds like a great idea! How beautiful!

Father JP: This struggle pleases God and purifies your love for your boyfriend. I'll tell you a little secret. I say a similar background prayer, but being a man I find it easier to address it to Our Lady, the mother of Jesus. I say, "Mary, may I only have eyes for you. May I only have a heart for Jesus."

Of course a non-Catholic Christian could address this prayer to Jesus; a non-Christian could address it to God; a married woman could employ her husband's name, as well, and a married man, his wife's. This is what love is all about: struggling to

His pects are a 9... No way, only an 8.5...
Oh, how sick — May I only have eyes for...!

dominate our natural tendencies and to orient them toward the good of those we love.

Margie: I think I could do that.

Loving Christ in the Other

Father JP: You may also try to turn your courtship with Sam and your signs of affection for him into a courtship with Christ. Tell Our Lord in your prayer — especially prayer before you go out with Sam — that you love Him and that you want to love Him through Sam. Tell Our Lord that every sign of affection for Sam is really for Him. When Sam says sweet and pleasant things to you, try addressing Our Lord with the same words that Sam addressed to you. Besides, everything you do for Sam can be an act of love for Our Lord. So Sam can actually help you feel the very presence of Our Lord in him.

If you work at trying to find Christ in Sam, then you won't be so tempted to selfishly seek yourself and indulge your sensuality.

44

Margie: This could transform our relationship. But isn't there a danger that my behavior might become a little stiff and artificial to Sam?

Father JP: Only if your relationship with Our Lord is stiff and artificial. This should help you have a more natural and affectionate relationship with Christ too. He doesn't want to have a stilted relationship with us.

This way of struggling works not only with passions for love and sexual pleasure, but with other inclinations too, such as anger or excessive concern for material possessions. If these tendencies dominate us, they destroy our relationships with those we love. True love moves us to discover our weaknesses and fight against them. Although we never completely rid ourselves of these tendencies, the harder we try, the more satisfying our relationships become.

Margie: I think this will help a lot, Father, especially from becoming sad when these feelings make me feel dirty, selfish, and empty.

Father JP: You're on the right track. Try to remember that it is not the thoughts or sensations that matter, but how we react to them. If we react by rejecting the temptation we do not sin but make a great affirmation of love.

Impure Dreams

Margie: But what about those impure dreams? Sometimes they just happen to occur in the middle of the night. They can be quite disturbing. Are they sinful?

Father JP: The dreams themselves are not sinful because we have no control over them. However, if we awake to impure dreams and give in to them, then they are no longer dreams. At this point, they may become sinful or they may not, depending on how one reacts to them.

Margie: How can you tell whether you are still dreaming or awake enough to sin?

Father JP: As I said, the dreams themselves are not sinful. As we begin to wake up from a dream, our intellect becomes aware of what is occurring in our imagination and body. It evaluates the dream, perhaps getting us to the point where we can say within ourselves, "Hey, this is an impure dream!" Still there is no sin.

After making this assessment, we come to a decision point: to allow this pleasurable event to continue in our mind or try to stop it. At this point, morality enters. If we react by struggling, we please God and say "I love you!" If we give in, then we sin.

When we reach that decision point, we should react and pray. Prayer shows God where our heart really is. It also provides us a source of grace and strength to resist by perhaps getting up, walking around, or finding something to distract our attention.

Margie: But sometimes my reaction is delayed, which makes it hard to tell whether I've given in or not.

Father JP: Don't worry, Margie. As you struggle in this, you will learn to discern the different stages. Reacting to the dreams will become easier, almost automatic. If you have any questions, bring them up in future confessions and I'll suggest other ways to struggle. Remember, when the struggle is positive, it pleases God.

Margie: That makes sense, but what about when I wake up and feel as though I may have compromised with a dream. Usually I'm kind of fuzzy about whether I was conscious enough to react. That yucky feeling just doesn't seem to go away. Should I still go to Communion if I feel this way?

Father JP: Don't go by your feelings. Feelings often fool us. If you are fuzzy about how conscious you are, then likely you are not conscious enough to commit a serious sin. Keep up the struggle when you are awake and don't worry about the feelings; they are probably just scruples that should be overcome with time.

Margie: Thank you, Father JP, I will.

Father JP: Thanks be to God.

The Logic of Love

Some weeks later, Sam and Margie returned to see Father JP. The couple had been thinking and talking with each other. Although Sam agreed with many points made in their previous session, he was not ready to concede. In fact, Sam was getting a little nervous about these sessions and was considering discontinuing them. So he decided to go to the main point that he came to discuss with Father JP and that he had hopes to convince Margie about. He really wanted this session to be the last.

What Is Love?

Sam: JP, thanks for getting together with us again. Last time you made a good point about how our eyes reflect the love in our hearts, or the lack thereof. I love Margie very much and I think she loves me too.

Margie: Yes, I do love you.

Sam: I don't think we have much of a problem reflecting that love with our eyes. The real issue is our desire to reflect that love sexually. You say sex is not dirty but a beautiful thing. However, to people like us — who love each other so completely and intensely — you say sex is wrong. If we really love each other and sex is so beautiful, how can it be wrong?

Father JP: You have a point. That is the most common reason unmarried couples give to justify having sex, but does that give them the right to do so?

Sam: Well, if they really love each other, what's wrong with it? In fact, it really seems like it is the right thing to do.

Father JP: But there is a more basic question we should consider first, that is: *what is love?*

Sam (*Obviously this question takes Sam by surprise, and he takes a few silent moments to think before replying.*):JP, that's a difficult question. My first thought is to say that love entails a strong emotional attraction that draws you to want to spend all your available time with the person you love. Love also means wishing that person well at all times. But to define *love* as such, that's hard.

Margie: I remember discussing this with a college roommate. For her love was just a good feeling you get when you're with someone you like. I found that so superficial. In Sunday school we were taught that God is Love. So true love must respect God and His commandments.

Sam: But that's not a definition. It's just impossible to define such a basic concept as *love.*

Father JP: Well, do you mind if we try? If we can understand the "metaphysics" of love, it would certainly make our task easier.

Sam: OK. Where do we start?

Father JP: To start, we should ask whether love is something physical or something spiritual. The obvious answer is spiritual because if not, God couldn't love because *God is spirit* (John 4:24). Yet we humans are physical and emotional beings, therefore we manifest our love in physical ways, sometimes arousing strong, emotional reactions. However, that doesn't mean that love itself is physical or emotional.

But if love is something fundamentally spiritual, then what is it?

Margie: How about unconditional self-giving?

Father JP: Love begins with unconditional self-giving, but love is more than that because self-giving can be one-directional. True love is mutual. It is only achieved when the person loved corresponds with his or her own self-giving.

True, complete love engenders a spiritual union of two people. When two people are strongly attracted to each other, each deciding to make a gift of him- or herself to the other, then *the fruit of that mutual self-giving is a spiritual union, or love;* the two become one spirit. Subsequently they begin to want the same thing and think in the same manner; they no longer live for themselves, but for the unity of the two. Pope John Paul says a loving couple has one "life project," living for a common goal. And as their love grows, the bond that ties these two spirits together becomes tighter and tighter.

Sam: If love is a spiritual union, fruit of a mutual self-giving, then it must be reciprocal. But what if I loved Margie and she didn't love me back?

Margie: And what about when God loves us and we don't love Him back? We are also asked to love our enemies who obviously don't reciprocate.

Father JP: You are both referring to unrequited love. Such love is one directional but calls for reciprocation. Obviously, Sam, if Margie did not respond to your love for her, then it would be frustrated because no union would be achieved without her self-giving.

God's love for us is best reflected in the Trinity, but we can also see it reflected in the family. A good father loves a child as a gift, as a unique creation that reflects his wife and their mutual self-gift. Likewise, a good mother loves a child for himself and as the personification of the physical and spiritual union with her husband. This love is not frustrated with a child's lack of love because it transcends the child, reaching the other spouse. Thus, God the Father loves each person as a father loves a child, seeing His only begotten Son reflected in each of us. Christ shows us that there is no greater love for a friend than to lay down one's life for him. As God and man, He did this by dying on the cross for us.

Likewise, when we love our enemy for love of God, it is God whom we love, expressing our unconditional, mutual, and reciprocal self-giving. That is why Our Lord says, *anything you do for the least of my brethren, you do for me* (Matthew 25:40). This imitates God the Son, who loves us as a brother, spouse (Ephesians 5:25–32), and mother (Matthew 12:50), drawing us into His union with the Father. The Holy Spirit personifies this union as the source of the new, divine life within us.

Therefore, if we always base our love for others on our love for God, ultimately our love will never be frustrated.

Margie: But a mother's love for her child is so total, self-sacrificing, and unconditional. How can you say that it is incomplete?

Father JP: As deep and real as that love may be, the mother-child love is not the same as spousal love. A couple shares very intimate personal communication of their deepest hopes and aspirations, hidden fears and anxieties, exposing their most intimate and vulnerable side to each other. This intimacy is exclusive. The life project is only shared between the spouses, for the child will go off — God willing — to form his or her own life project with someone else. Thus, the mother-child relationship is incomplete and could only be complete if it included the intimate communication and sharing of the life project found in spousal love. Mother-child love only participates in and expresses the complete spousal love.

Sam: What about the guy who loves a girl who doesn't love him back? He may even respect the fact that she loves someone else. He keeps his stance so she can be happy with the man she has chosen. Doesn't this man love fully?

Father JP: This man may be called to give himself to another. He may ignore another woman yearning for his love due to his attachment to the first. Remaining attached to one who has chosen to love another can be selfish when one fails to open oneself up to possibly love someone else.

In any case, when someone loves another with openness to total self-giving but is rebuffed, then that love will always be incomplete, incapable of communicating one's deepest hopes and fears with the other.

Sam: And if one of the parties frustrates that love by infidelity or abuse?

Father JP: Sam, it would be the same. Whenever a relationship lacks self-giving from either person, then mere human love will be frustrated. That is why it is so important to base our human love on love for God, because God — as Moses writes — "is a faithful God" (Deuteronomy 7:9). He never disappoints (Psalm 22:5; Romans 5:5).

A husband may be unfaithful by having an affair, but if his wife's love is directed toward God through her husband, then her faithful love is not wasted. A person may be married to an alcoholic, to a verbally abusive spouse, or to one with psychological problems due to childhood abuse. On the human side, such love seems frustrated and disappointing, but supernaturally love reaches incomparable heights because of the complete, self-sacrificing, and heroic nature of the person's self-giving.

Margie: But isn't that unrequited love?

Father JP: On the human side, yes it is. However, one's love for God transcends human weakness and infidelity, allowing a person to achieve perfect love. Nevertheless, we should all strive that our human love reflects our love for God.

Language of the Body

Sam: But according to Judaism, we're not pure spirits. We are physical beings, too.

Father JP: Yes, we have a body. Our body is intimately joined to our soul. In fact, they are so closely united that everything spiritual about us must be expressed in a physical way.

For instance, our thoughts are spiritual but because we are human, we must express them physically. How do we express our spiritual thoughts and desires?

Margie: With words, of course.

Father JP: Right! Sometimes we express those thoughts with vocal words — physical air vibrations that we make with our mouth and vocal cords. Sometimes we express them with written words marked out by ink splotches on a piece of paper. Other times we use some other kind of physical gesture. Yet all of these physical expressions manifest and communicate our spiritual thoughts and desires.

Sam: Would that include e-mail?

Father JP: You bet! Even the digital ones and zeros sent between computers are physical realities that transmit our spiritual thoughts.

Love too is a spiritual reality that needs to be expressed in a physical way.

Margie: You mean love is also expressed by physical words.

Father JP: Love goes beyond words. Words are limited since they only can express the thoughts and desires of the individual, whereas love goes beyond the individual to express something common between two persons.

So how do mortal, physical beings like us express the spiritual reality of love?

Margie: By service and self-giving.

Father JP: Those things are important, but there are some very special ways of expressing the union of spirits found in love, and that is by a union of bodies. The spiritual union may be expressed by a physical handshake or by holding hands; by a hug or a kiss; or finally, by the sexual union of bodies. All of

You are so beautiful to me!

these are physical expressions of a spiritual reality: a union of bodies expressing a union of spirits.

Margie: That makes a lot of sense.

Sam: Yes, it does. You have defined the "indefinable" quite well. Love, as a spiritual union expressed by a union of bodies, is a very beautiful way of defining love. JP, I think you have demonstrated precisely the point I have been trying to make all along, that it is OK for Margie and me, or any couple, to have sex as long as we truly love each other, since sex is a beautiful expression of this spiritual union that we have.

Father JP: Hold on, Sam, we are not quite finished here. Not all physical expressions of love are appropriate.

For example, Sam, do you love your mother?

Sam: Yes.

Father JP: Does that mean you express your love for her sexually?

Sam: God forbid! But that's a different kind of love. The love I have for my mother is very different from the love I have for Margie.

Father JP: But what's that difference? You may hug your mother, hold her hand and give her a kiss. These physical unions of bodies manifest the spiritual union between you and her appropriately. What makes the sexual union different?

Sam: I don't know, but it is certainly different.

Father JP: The difference between the sexual union and a hug is quite simple: its totality! In the conjugal act between a man and a woman each person gives his or her whole body totally to the other without holding anything back, without hiding anything. And there is no shame in this, even in one's unclothed body. In short, the sexual union is the most complete union of bodies possible that takes place through the total gift of one's body to the other. This totality does not take place with a hug or a kiss.

So what should the physical totality of the sexual union express spiritually?

Margie: A complete union of spirits?

Father JP: Exactly. Although you love your mother and father immensely, your love for them is not total. Nor is their love for you total and complete, as their love ought to be for each other; this is why incest is so detestable.

There even exists a kind of spiritual incest. It sometimes happens that a parent will confide with an older child certain intimate details of his or her relationship with a spouse, or even with an extramarital partner. No matter how old the child is, when a parent makes a child a confidant, he or she spoils the child's relationship with both parents, forcing the child to take sides and become their judge.

Now, getting back to the subject of the two of you. How would you react, Margie, if Sam approached you one evening and said,

"Margie, I really love you. My spirit wants to give itself completely to you. I don't want to hold anything back; I don't want to hide anything from you — but just for tonight. What do you say, can we do it?"

Margie: No way!

Father JP: Why?

Margie: Because it would be so temporary and incomplete.

Father JP: But if Sam came back and said, "But, Margie, I really do love you. I really do want to give myself completely to you, without holding anything back and hiding anything — but just for the next six months, now what do you say, can we do it?" Would that be enough?

Margie: Still, no way.

Father JP: And if he said, "I do want to spiritually give myself to you for as long as things work out. How about that?"

Margie: No. Something is still missing. It's not complete.

Father JP: How about, "I want to spiritually give myself to you completely, really completely, forever, until death do us part"?

Margie: Yeah. That is complete.

Father JP: But what do we call that? What do we call the mutual, lifetime commitment to give oneself spiritually to another, without holding anything back, without hiding anything, unconditionally until death do them part?

Margie: Marriage.

Father JP: You got it! The sexual union is a physical expression of the total spiritual union of two people that we find in marriage.

So what does having sex outside of marriage mean? What does it say? What do you have when a couple physically express one thing but they mentally or spiritually mean something else?

Sam: It means they are not being honest with each other.

56

Father JP: Yes, you could put it that way. You could also call it by its name — a lie. The Pope describes it in this way:

> *The total physical self-giving would be a lie if it were not the sign and fruit of a total personal self-giving, in which the whole person, including the temporal dimension, is present: If the person were to withhold something or reserve the possibility of deciding otherwise in the future, by this very fact he or she would not be giving totally.*[5]

Sam: But not all lies are that bad.

Father JP: All lies are evil because they are deceptive, making us in a sense children of Satan, the "father of lies" (John 8:44). Lies destroy the mutual trust needed in every relationship. If we don't know what another person intends to say by his actions or words, then we don't know where we truly stand in our relationship to him, making us a prime target for being taken advantage of.

But even if you could say that some lies were not serious, this one is particularly grievous and destructive.

Sam: How so? We're talking about a couple that love each other even though they are not ready for an enduring commitment. Besides, it is a mutual decision to have sex. So why is it such a big deal?

Father JP: Sam, I know this is difficult, but let's think: what is lost when the lie is the sexual union between two people who are not married?

Sam: You mean, virginity? That is no longer an issue for me.

Father JP: No, there is something more than just the loss of "physical" virginity, although that is important to many people. Let's look at another example to explain my point.

Suppose you were looking to buy a car and you happened upon one advertised for sale on the side of the road. You stop to check it out; you take the car for a spin, kick the tires, and then start haggling with the owner over the price. The two of you settled on a price, let's say 5,000 dollars. Then what do you do?

Sam: Sign the papers and drive the car home.

Father JP: Before that — at the moment you reached agreeable terms — wouldn't you shake hands, or something?

Sam: Yeah, I guess I would.

Father JP: Shaking hands is an expression of your union of wills. Granted, it is a very limited union of wills, but still, we express that spiritual union with a union of bodies. But notice you don't give the guy a kiss, do you?

Sam: Of course not.

Father JP: That is because a kiss would be an inappropriate expression of this union of wills, which is so limited and temporal. In fact, we don't normally call this *love* at all, because this union of wills is so partial. Nevertheless, this is a union of spirits.

So after shaking hands you give him the cash and he signs the title of the car over to you and hands you the keys. But just as you were about ready to drive off, he says, "Sam, it just occurred to me: every time there is an exchange of title, you have to get a smog check and certificate for the car. If you like — because it can be quite a hassle — I know a mechanic at the garage down the street, I could take the car there for you and save you the hassle." Let's say you agree, since you hate to hassle with mechanics.

Sam: Actually, you're right, I don't like to bother with those kinds of things.

Father JP: OK, so you went home and then returned the next day only to discover the car not there, nor the man who sold you the car, nor the cash that you gave him. In the end, what was the value of that exchange of hands?

Sam: It was a lie.

It's a deal!

Father JP: Even though you had a satisfying feeling at the moment you shook hands? You had the great feeling of having getting a great price on a very good car. But after the fact, didn't you feel different about it?

Sam: Well, at the time we shook hands, the deal had not turned bad, nor had I lost 5,000 dollars cash. But if I were swindled out of that amount of money, I'd be pretty angry.

Father JP: In this hypothetical lie, you would have lost a few dollars and been angry for a few hours. Perhaps you would be less likely to trust others in business.

But in the case of two people engaging in sexual relations before marriage, what you lose is not just a few dollars but the very gift of yourself, your identity as a person and your ability to give of yourself completely and exclusively to the person you choose to love for life. Although the two may mutually agree and feel good while having sexual relations, it actually leaves each empty of what is most intimate and personal. It also makes it more difficult to trust another person completely with one's life.

But he shook my hand...

Margie: I can attest to that. I felt so bad after being intimate with a guy, and we didn't even go all the way. I felt the pain and the shame of losing something very personal and intimate, something that was part of my very being. I felt that I'd lost something that I couldn't get back, that I was now unable to give to my love.

Sam: But I don't think everybody feels "empty" or "bad" after having sex.

Father JP: No, of course not. In fact, most married people find it is a most wonderful and meaningful experience.

Sam: I mean for those having sex before marriage, I don't think they necessarily feel "empty" or "bad." Otherwise, why would they keep doing it?

Father JP: They keep doing it because it gives them intense sexual gratification. A better question to ask is whether or not their having sex is being done for selfish motives. Certainly some men have no problem frequenting prostitutes, because all they are interested in is selfish sexual gratification. They don't seem to feel "empty" or "bad" either because the intensity of the selfish gratification gradually masks the shame and the sense of personal loss. But it doesn't mask that shame completely; few men who go to prostitutes are proud of it. They rarely brag about it. Those who are have become quite hardened.

Sam: I think you're exaggerating the point I was trying to make. Many feel that sex is a fun, special, and, yes, very pleasurable experience that they share with another person they love. They see it as something that strengthens their relationship.

Father JP: Sam, I didn't mean to exaggerate your position. However, if lust and selfishness motivate the sexual activity, then it cannot truly be fulfilling nor strengthen a relationship. You cannot base a loving relationship on selfishness even if the selfishness is mutual.

Sam: But you imply that just because it is done outside of marriage, sexual activity must be motivated by selfishness and lust. I don't think that's always the case.

Father JP: Our motivation is often a mix of selfish interests and altruistic concerns. But since human sexuality is so closely linked to the most intimate dimensions of the human person, we must do the utmost to protect it from any possibility of being abused by selfishness and lust.

But let's leave this here for a moment. I think it'll make more sense as we go along.

Physically the extramarital sexual union does indeed express, "I am all yours, I give myself completely to you without holding anything back; I accept your gift of yourself to me just as you are, completely and unconditionally, without any limits; we are completely one." Nevertheless, it is still a deceitful lie because it does not reflect the spiritual reality of a full commitment before God and the world. It doesn't respect the totality of the gift that the other person is expressing.

Marriage: Just a Piece of Paper?

Sam: But if two people are engaged, they have already committed themselves to a lifetime union and have complete trust in each other's binding love. Why is it so wrong for them to have sex before having their marriage blessed?

Father JP: By becoming engaged, a couple manifests their intention to make a lifetime commitment. However, the actual spiritual union and commitment between them has yet to be made. Either party could back out at any moment, even minutes before the wedding ceremony. Now in doing so, such a person may be a jerk for dragging things out so long, but he or she is still free to do so, both legally and morally.

Margie: Sam, I think I see Father's point: sex is a beautiful thing, the perfect physical reflection of what takes place spiritually.

Sam: Must the sexual love *only* reflect complete commitment? We're mature enough to determine the level of commitment appropriate for sex for us. As long as it authentically expresses our feelings of love, that should be sufficient. Why must we use your definition?

Father JP: Do you really want to start redefining what sex means? If so, then why stop there? We could also start redefining what traffic signals mean. If that is our choice, we won't live very long. Besides, how much commitment to Margie do you want this act to express — a day, a month, as long as things work out?

(Father JP sees how Margie is beginning to react.) Now, Margie, we are just speaking hypothetically.

Margie: I understand, Father JP, but let's face it, we're not talking about some hypothetical relationship. Ultimately we are talking about the relationship between Sam and me.

Father JP: Very true, Margie. That is why it is important that we have this conversation.

Sam: But, JP, isn't getting married really just a legality? The wedding is just a ritual and the marriage license is just a piece of paper. What's really important is the love and commitment in the heart of the two who are getting married.

Father JP: What is in the heart is totally important. However, love can blind the heart from seeing reality. The wedding and the marriage covenant are there to protect each person, the family, and the institution of marriage.

Think about it, Sam, would you loan a friend a large sum of money, or buy or sell a house just based on the other person's word?

Sam: No, that would be somewhat foolish.

Father JP: It certainly would. You'd be a prime target for someone taking advantage of you. Our society encourages and enforces contracts to protect innocent people and to foster the kind of trust necessary for a real business economy to occur.

The same with marriage: it is a covenant instituted to foster an environment of trust necessary for lasting love and family, especially to protect each person and their potential children from being taken advantage of by the other. It also helps those considering marriage to realize beforehand how special and serious this commitment is. When you sign on the dotted line — when you say, "I do" — you know that you will be held to your word.

Why No Divorce?

Sam: OK, you're right. But if sex is such a beautiful thing that must wait for marriage, then the Catholic Church shouldn't prohibit divorce. If two people get married and then find themselves sexually incompatible — with no option of divorce — then that's it; say "good-bye" to that beautiful expression of love. If they could have sex before marriage then they could at least discover this incompatibility before making a lifelong mistake.

Father JP: The prohibition against divorce is not a Catholic thing. Even the Jewish Scripture condemned it:

63

You cover the Lord's altar with tears, with weeping and groaning. . . . Because the Lord was witness to the covenant between you and the wife of your youth, to whom you have been faithless, though she is your companion and your wife by covenant. . . . So take heed to yourselves, and let none be faithless to the wife of his youth. "For I hate divorce, says the Lord, the God of Israel. . . . So take heed to yourselves and do not be faithless." (Malachi 2:13–16)

Sam: Still, if a couple cannot find out whether they are compatible or not before marrying, then they need a way out if things don't really work.

Father JP: That kind of discovery should take place before marriage. Perhaps the most important thing the couple needs to discover is whether there is unconditional love on both sides. Am I right on this?

Sam: That seems reasonable, especially if it allows for the proper expression of that unconditional love!

Father JP: But, Sam, what better way for a couple to discover whether there is unconditional love between them, than to wait until marriage? This is especially true for the woman. This is how she knows that her guy loves her unconditionally.

Margie: Why especially for women? Doesn't waiting also show a woman's unconditional love?

Father JP: Yes, it does. However, men readily feign commitment in order to have sex. For them, waiting is generally more of a sacrifice. Women generally feel bonded to their man without sex, whereas men bond less easily.

Moreover, the woman has more to risk; if she gets pregnant, she then has a child to care for. The man can walk away, and often does. So it is generally safer and easier for women to wait than it is for men.

Sam: But you say waiting and not having sex before marriage is a sign of love, but after the wedding such waiting is not. I

64

think you are just trying to define things to get the results that you want.

Father JP: That's not what I intend. The issue is how does a person know that the other person is really committed to the relationship? How does one know whether one's partner's love is unconditional?

Would a couple's love be unconditional if they stipulated having marital relations with a minimum frequency? What if after years of marriage they could no longer have sex, for example, because she contracted an illness making the union impossible or life threatening? If a man refused to marry his girlfriend foreseeing these conditions, or subsequently divorced his wife when they occurred, would he really love her unconditionally?

Sam: No, of course not, but that presupposes an ideal world. If you don't have any physical intimacy before marriage, then you have no knowledge of what it will be like or how you and the other person match; that requires having sex. Either you allow divorce or you allow premarital sex.

Father JP: What kind of incompatibility are you concerned about? Physical? A doctor could answer that.

Sam: No, but whether the couple has the right "chemistry."

Father JP: If you mean by "chemistry" that the two are attracted to each other, they don't need to have sex to discover that.

You seem to presume their sex life is the reason why most couples divorce. It rarely is. "Chemistry" usually refers to the emotional side of how well a couple communicates and shares the deeper, more intimate aspects of their beings. The reason why most people divorce is because they have a lot of issues they haven't worked out before marriage. How will he or she treat me when we are married? How will he or she handle a financial crisis, arguments, and his or her anger? When shall we have children and how many? What kind of relationship are we going to maintain with each other's family? How will we practice religion in the family and as a family?

Oh, the Chemistry of Love

These and other similar issues are the main reasons for conflict in marriage. If a dating couple spends their time and energy on physical intimacy, they often ignore or fail to explore their compatibility issues.

It is true that these issues may have repercussions on a couple's sexual intimacy. If a husband is selfish about not helping around the house, he may fall into seeking his own sexual gratification selfishly. Or the other way around, if a man gets his selfish needs met sexually, he is less likely to be generous in other areas such as helping around the house. If a wife feels that her husband is not holding up his end of the bargain financially, she is less likely to want to be there for him sexually.

When things become overly physical, one easily gets caught up in the sexual or romantic dimension of the relationship. Emphasis is put on "performance" and looking for opportunities for going further. There is less talk about what really matters to marriage. A couple would benefit more by exploring each other's likes and dislikes, interests and hobbies, or what each desires in forming a family and having children — their life values and religious convictions. These things are what matter on a day-to-day basis in a marriage. Yet physically involved couples often fear addressing such topics, because they are potentially disruptive to the relationship and the physical intimacies. This fear impedes true communication about matters important to marital compatibilities.

Sam: But shouldn't a person who finds him- or herself married with incompatibility issues like the ones you mentioned get a second chance?

Father JP: The logic of love answers this question.

Sam: How so?

Father JP: Let's suppose you and I were very good friends. I was in a good mood one day and decided to give you a hundred dollars out of appreciation for you and your friendship, saying, "Use it in any way you wish. I want you to enjoy yourself."
If I did this for you, how would you react?

Sam: It would be a bit odd — I can't imagine any of my friends ever doing this. But if you and I were great friends and you were generous in this way, I guess I'd be grateful and look for a way to somehow return the favor.

Father JP: Let's say then that I give you this little gift. A few weeks later I come up to you and say, "Hey, where's my hundred dollars?"
You'd probably reply, "But wait a minute, JP, you gave it to me as a gift."
But I reply, "I know, but now I want it back. Sorry."

Sam: A gift is a gift. To take it back means it was never a gift. Besides, I may have spent the money on something that wasn't in my budget, thinking that you had given it to me unconditionally. Then I'd be in a real predicament because I wouldn't have the money to pay you back. If you did that, you wouldn't be my friend anymore — that's for sure.

Father JP: Exactly! When a person gives himself to another in marriage his love is a real gift, a gift of his very self. If at some point he changes his mind and decides to take it back, he becomes a real scoundrel. It's as though he never really meant to give himself. And the other person is now in a predicament, having given herself to him thinking the gift was mutual. She has spent her gift on him while he chooses to be a selfish scoundrel.

Sam: And if they both agree to call it quits and give back their gifts of themselves?

Father JP: A gift is still a gift, as you said. That the two of them jointly decide to rescind their unconditional and lifetime gift of themselves only makes them both selfish scoundrels. Then both are saying their gifts were never gifts at all.

Margie: But what if things really get ugly in the marriage, for instance, the husband is unfaithful?

Father JP: God has made the marriage covenant permanent. However, a couple may separate if there is infidelity or danger of physical or emotional harm to the innocent party or children.

Sam: But isn't that only for Catholics?

Father JP: Not so, Sam. By establishing a marital covenant with the people of Israel, God showed us his plan for marriage.

In the Hebrew Scriptures Israel was frequently unfaithful to the covenant, prostituting itself by worshiping other gods. When Israel refused to rectify its infidelity, God allowed other nations to overrun their land, even to the point of uprooting them and carrying them off into captivity in Babylon. But God was still faithful to His covenant.

In other words, God permitted a separation between Him and His spouse, Israel, but He allowed her to come back when the people repented of their sin. Please read Psalm 106, which summarizes God's marital relationship to his people who "played the harlot," while He remained faithful to the covenant.

Sam: I have to admit, there is a kind of logic to all this. But not everyone in our society looks at things this way. I don't know if this logic can be applied to everybody.

Father JP: We call this kind of logic the "logic of love."

Sam: I still have other questions though — like one about the Church's teaching on birth control. I don't see how it fits with your "logic of love."

Father JP: I am sure we'll get to these other questions as we continue meeting.

Margie: I look forward to that, Father JP. I hope Sam does too. This has been really interesting — and challenging.

Father JP: You're right, Margie, this has been a very good conversation. Both of you have made some very interesting and challenging comments and raised valid questions. I look forward to our next meeting myself.

Sam: I look forward to it, too.

Father JP: Well, until we meet next time.

The Eucharist and Spousal Love

The following Saturday, Margie returned to Father JP for confession. After confession, she asked Father JP a few questions.

Margie: Father JP, this is Margie. Do you mind if I ask you something?

Father JP: No Margie, go right ahead.

Margie: Father JP, I have to admit I have never seen or heard the Church's teaching on sexuality explained the way you did to us last week. Since returning to the Church, I've read some of the *Catechism of the Catholic Church*. Sam too has begun to read a few things in the *Catechism*. Your explanation sounds very nice, but where do we find it?

Father JP: This teaching on sexuality complements the mysteries of our Faith. It's amazing how the Church's teaching on marriage and sexuality conforms exactly to God's way of showing His love for us. God shows His love for us exactly the same way a man and a woman show their complete self-giving love, through a union of bodies.

Margie: How so? Do you mean to say that God wants to make love to us?

Father JP: Margie, I wouldn't say it quite that way, but in a sense you are right. Let me explain.

Christ has given us Eucharistic Communion. We believe that Jesus Christ, on the night before He was crucified and died on the Cross, took bread and wine and transformed it into His Body and Blood. He did this so that His followers could be united to Him. Through the priest, we believe that Christ continues to convert the bread and wine we offer at Holy Mass into His Body and Blood, so that we can consume Him. When we eat His Body we become physically united to Christ, we become one body with Him, expressing that union of spirits, that spiritual bond that ought to exist between Our Lord and us.

So there's a great parallel between the Eucharistic Communion and the marital union wherein a man and a woman become one body.

Margie: Father, isn't that a little sacrilegious?

Father JP: That's what I thought when this idea first occurred to me. But a few months later, I stumbled across it in the writings of Pope John Paul II. So if the Pope makes this connection, then it couldn't be that sacrilegious! This teaching is found in his Apostolic Letter, *On the Dignity and Vocation of Women,* in a chapter entitled "The Eucharist."

One may ask, what is a chapter on the Eucharist doing in a document on women and their vocation? Well, the Holy Father uses this document to explain the spousal relationship between God and His people, between Christ and His Church. And he quotes from St. Paul's Letter to the Ephesians, chapter 5: *Husbands love your wives as Christ loved the Church, and gave Himself up for her, that he might sanctify her.* St. Paul concludes this passage, saying, *"For this reason a man shall leave his father and mother and be joined to his wife, and the two*

Oh, how you love ME, Lord

shall become one flesh." This mystery is a profound one, and I am saying that it refers to Christ and the church (Ephesians 5:25–32).

The mystery of marriage and the one-flesh union of man and woman is a profound mystery or sacrament, expressing the relationship between Christ and the Church. Of course, this was all foreshadowed in the Old Testament.

And in the Pope's chapter on the Eucharist, we read:

Against the broad background of the "great mystery" expressed in the spousal relationship between Christ and the Church..., we find ourselves in the very heart of the Pascal Mystery, which completely reveals the spousal love of God. Christ is the bridegroom, because "he has given himself": his body has been "given," his blood has been "poured out" (cf. Luke 22:19–20). In this way "he loved them to the end" (John 13:1). The "sincere gift" [the gift of himself] contained in the Sacrifice of the Cross gives definitive prominence to the spousal meaning of God's love. The Redeemer of the world, Christ, is the bridegroom of the Church. The Eucharist is the Sacrament of our Redemption, it is the Sacrament of the Bridegroom and the Bride.... [Christ] "creates" the Church, his body, and unites [himself] with his "body," as the bridegroom with the bride....

It is the Eucharist, above all, that expresses the redemptive act of Christ, the Bridegroom, towards the Church, the Bride.[6]

Margie: So we become united to Christ in the Eucharist in a marital-type union.

Father JP: Yes! Since the Eucharist is the Body of Christ. When we receive Him in Communion, there is a spousal union of bodies. Christ gives us His whole Body; we receive Him in our body. He also calls us to give our body to Him completely. This mutual gift of our whole body to Christ and His to us brings about a perfect, total physical union, which expresses a real, total union of spirits.

Margie: Is this true for non-Catholics too? Do they share the same intimate union with Christ?

Father JP: They do have some kind of union with Christ because they believe in Him and are united to Him in prayer. However, non-Catholics should not receive sacramental Communion because if they did, they would physically receive Christ's body but without the spiritual union with Christ that comes with faith, Baptism, and full union with Christ's body, the Church. It would be like having the marital union without the marital commitment. That is why the Church has always taught that to receive

72

Communion, without the proper dispositions, is a serious sin of sacrilege.

A sacrilege is to show grave disrespect for something sacred. Well, what could be more sacred than God's own Body?

Margie: Then what are the proper dispositions to receive Communion?

Father JP: The first necessary disposition is to be baptized and profess the full Catholic Faith. In addition to faith and Baptism, Catholics must be in the state of grace. As the *Catechism of the Catholic Church* says:

> *Anyone who desires to receive Christ in Eucharistic communion must be in the state of grace. Anyone aware of having sinned mortally must not receive communion without having received absolution in the sacrament of penance.* (n. 1415. Cf. 1385, 1457)

Of course, we should always be well prepared in spirit and in body to receive such a great gift from God.

Margie: I didn't realize it was such a big deal to receive Communion. It is really something special.

Father JP: Do you now see how these things fit together so beautifully? This is why the Church does not consider human sexuality something bad or dirty, but something of great dignity, something sacred. The Church compares the marital union to what it holds most sacred, to the Eucharist, the Body and Blood of her Savior. And married couples, especially married Catholics and Christians, are called to express in their own marriage the sacrificial love that Christ has for the Church and the Church has for Christ. They give a wonderful witness to the world of Christ's great love, by loving one another as Christ loved the Church.

Margie: That is quite a challenge.

Father JP: Yes, it is, but God gives us the grace we need to carry out the mission to which He calls us. Receiving Communion is one of the best ways to prepare ourselves for whatever

God should ask of us. But let's work at receiving Him better, with less sin and with more love. It will bring you greater peace and purity of heart, and will also prepare you to discover and carry out your vocation, whether to marriage or some other form of dedication to God.

Margie: Are you saying that marriage is a vocation?

Father JP: Yes. Marriage is a vocation to witness to the Gospel, to the spousal relationship between Christ and His Church. A married couple is called to exemplify that love, so that the people who see the couple's love for each other will be attracted to the Christ who inspires their love. If more couples and families lived this vocation generously and heroically, more people would be attracted to Christ and His family, the Church.

Margie: I could imagine that a witness of a good married couple could be quite valuable today, since good families are so rare. It is also a very attractive challenge.

Father JP: Keep up your efforts to deepen your prayer life, especially receiving better and more frequently Our Lord in Communion, and you will prepare yourself for living out such a challenge, if God calls you to that.

Margie: Thank you, Father.

Father JP: You're welcome. I look forward to seeing you and Sam soon.

The Meaning of Contraception

A week or so later, Sam and Margie meet again with Father JP. Sam wants to follow up on the promised topic of contraception. He thinks this is the one topic where the Catholic Church has it all wrong. Sam also thinks that Father JP may have been deliberately avoiding this topic.

Contraception and Overpopulation

Sam: JP, thanks for meeting with us again. You've certainly given us a lot to think about.

Father JP: I'm glad you take love so seriously.

Sam: Yet a topic we seem to have avoided is contraception. It seems to me that the Catholic Church is not concerned about overpopulation. The world's population keeps increasing, but the Earth just can't handle all the people that are being born. We are running out of resources and the environment is being abused. Don't you think it is irresponsible of us not to use contraception to prevent the world's population from getting out of hand?

Father JP: Sam, I'm glad that you're so concerned about the world and the environment. I wish more people were as concerned as you are. We do have an obligation to take care of this gift that God has given us and to pass it on in good shape to those who will follow us. Certainly the world's population ought to be a concern; we would be irresponsible if we were to neglect it.

But is that the real issue here?

Sam: What do you mean? The issue seems quite clear; we must use all the means in our power to protect the world for future generations. Contraception is indispensable to protect the environment from too many people being born.

Father JP: Maybe the issues are not as clear as you think they are.

Instead of contraception, suppose we used a different method to control the population. For instance, one way we could do this would be to terminate everyone over sixty years old. People over sixty are less productive; they tend to get sick and consume more medical and economic resources; their technical skills are no longer up to date; also, they've had their chance to enjoy life and do something good with it. Why should we prevent younger people from coming into the world who can more easily learn new skills and technology? Younger people also tend to be more productive in the workforce. Why eliminate those who have not yet had a chance to show what they can do with their lives?

Sam: What are you proposing to do?

Father JP: Well, society could establish a law that the state would terminate the lives of all men and women when they reach their sixtieth birthday. If that would not fully eliminate the population problem, then we can always lower the age until it does. This would be real population control.

Margie: But that would be immoral.

Sam: I agree. I would never go along with that. Many people are still productive at sixty and beyond. To kill them off would be a real crime.

Father JP: That's my point. Morality is an important consideration when evaluating the means to control population. So, before we consider using contraception to control over-population, we must ascertain its moral value. If contraception is immoral, then we cannot use it even though the end—to preserve the world's beauty and resources for future generations—is very noble.

What Does Contraception "Say?"

Sam: JP, you have stated that the Church thinks very highly of human sexuality, that it is the ultimate sign of love between a man and woman in marriage. But there are cases where it would be unwise or even dangerous for a married woman to have another child. Contraception enables a couple to continue to express their love for each other in this "sacred" manner while avoiding the grave risk to the woman's life. Yet the Church still condemns it.

Margie: Father, Sam challenged me with this argument a while back. I told him that God designed sex for making babies. Any sex not open to children would thwart God's designs. As you see, Sam is not convinced and I'm not fully convinced either.

Sam: But there are couples that are sterile: must they avoid sex since it cannot produce children? Or are couples too old to have children also to abstain? With or without faith, this seems to project a negative view of sexuality.

Besides, the same thing could be applied to cancer — cancer is natural, so science shouldn't manipulate the body in order to eliminate this deadly disease. Nobody goes for that any longer, except for a few quacks. So, if we can manipulate the body to improve our health, why can't we manipulate it to regulate fertility?

Margie: You just need faith to understand this teaching.

Sam: Then only Catholics would be prohibited from using contraceptives. Non-Catholics are not bound by the religious teachings of the Church.

Father JP: Both of you make some interesting and valid points. Yes, faith makes it easier to accept this teaching, but really it is part of basic moral principles accessible to all. Contraception is right or wrong independent of faith.

The problem is, however, if a person is stuck in his or her own pride and not open to accept this teaching, then no matter how powerful the argument may be, that person will not accept it. We are free beings capable of rejecting moral principles, no matter how basic or obvious.

The morality of contraception has less to do with not having children and more to do with its implications on love, implications that apply to everybody.

Sam: Just as I was saying, Margie. I knew I was right on this one. JP isn't old-fashioned. Conception is about love, not about having more or less children.

Father JP: Sam, let's not jump the gun here. Margie was right on one point, that God has linked the procreation of children to human love and sexuality. *What therefore God has joined together, let not man put asunder* (Mark 10:9). If we are to respect what God has joined together in the sexual act, then life will be the fruit of love, and love will always be open to life. Whatever a person does to stomp out that life, or keep it from coming into being, will result in stomping out love.

Margie: See, Sam, I was right.

Father JP: Now let's calm down. To understand this teaching we need to lay aside our emotions and look at things objectively. Unless we can do that, there is no use discussing this further. Are you ready to do that?

Margie: Yes, Father, I am. I'm sorry.

Father JP: And you, Sam?

Sam: I'll give it my best. But these are deep emotional issues that reflect both what love is as well as who we are as persons.

Father JP: You're correct, Sam. But we need to have a level head to reach the true nature of love. If we are open, then we will discover what the truth is.

Sam: Like I said, JP, I'll try.

Father JP: To start, let's ask ourselves, what does contraception say? In other words, what does contraception do to the sexual act, to that expression of total mutual self-giving? Does it change the meaning of the act?

Sam: As I see it, what contraception does is prevent the conception of a child without interrupting the union of bodies. And, as we discussed earlier, that union of bodies fully expresses the union of spirits.

Margie: I don't know if I agree. Contraception seems to do something. It is just not the same, but I can't really say why.

Father JP: Let me use an example that should help clarify our perspective on this.

Let's say that the two of you were together and beginning to get romantic. You were cuddling up on a park bench. Sam put his arm around your shoulder, Margie, and as you, Sam, were turning to give Margie a kiss, she stopped you, put her purse in her lap, and pulled out a piece of plastic wrap. Then she put the plastic wrap over her lips and said, "OK, Sam, now you can kiss me. I just don't want to get your germs."

Sam: I wouldn't kiss her after that.

Father JP: Why not? What would Margie be saying by putting plastic wrap over her lips?

Sam: Maybe she would be saying that her health was more important to her than I was.

Margie: It certainly wouldn't say, "I love you."

Father JP: Yet the sexual union is much more intimate than a kiss. So how can a couple ever put a barrier in between them in that most intimate of moments? Do you really think that one can use contraception without affecting what the sexual act says?

Margie: No, of course not. Contraception really does make a difference!

Safe-Sex ... Safe-Kiss

Father JP: Yes, it does. It changes the whole nature of the sexual act. Contraception interrupts and prevents the total gift of self that the communion of bodies is meant to express. A contraceptive act is not a total gift of self. It does not say, "I give my whole self to you and accept your gift of self to me unconditionally," because contraception puts conditions on the gift of self. "I will give you everything — everything except my fertility." This is not unconditional love. As you suggested, it would

be like saying, "Not having children is more important than y
are to me, than the totality of our self-giving."

In fact, when a couple uses a barrier to prevent conception,
they put a physical wall between the two of them. This has profound psychological and spiritual repercussions, often causing
the couple to become more distant from each other, to see each
other as an object of pleasure rather than a subject of total self-
giving. Each individual is more interested in what he or she is
going to get out of the sexual act and not what it means. It is
no wonder that divorce is so prevalent among contracepting
spouses.

Sam: Are you trying to tell me that divorce is greater among
couples using contraception?

Father JP: The current divorce rate is about 50 percent. However, couples using Natural Family Planning instead of contraception have a divorce rate between 1 and 5 percent.[7]

Margie: That's quite a difference.

Father JP: But it makes sense if you understand how contraception puts severe conditions on one's self-giving, changing
the meaning of the sexual act.

Sam: I don't see the necessary link between a lower divorce
rate and Natural Family Planning. The people who use Natural
Family Planning are much more likely to be in a religion that
prohibits divorce than the public at large. Statistics can distort
reality.

Father JP: You may be right, Sam, but other studies seem to
establish a clear link between the increase of the divorce rate
with the increased use of contraceptives by married couples.[8]

Isn't Natural Family Planning the Same as Contraception?

Sam: But the Church allows the rhythm method. Isn't it the
same as contraception? In both cases, it is the couple — not

81

God — who chooses whether a child should enter the world. In one case, they use a condom or pill; in the other, they abstain from sex during the woman's fertile periods. The Church seems to be inconsistent here because both methods have the same results.

Father JP: Yet they are not the same. You cannot judge the morality of an action just by looking at the results. If they were the same, more people would use Natural Family Planning because it is natural and has fewer side effects.

Sam: Well, you're right. They aren't quite the same: Natural Family Planning takes much more sacrifice and is not as effective. But why put oneself through that extra pain when you don't have to?

Father JP: Scientific studies show Natural Family Planning to be as effective as or more than most forms of contraception. It does require more sacrifice, but sacrifice manifests true love and mutual respect for each other as persons. It is this love and respect that motivates couples to make that sacrifice.

The morality of contraception is not judged by the results or ends of the action — in our case, avoiding having another child — but by the means or methods and by what those means say. The end does not justify the means. Let's go back to our example we were using before.

Let's say that the two of you were again cuddling up together, getting romantic. You, Sam, turn to give Margie a kiss when she stops you and says, "No, Sam. I have this horrible cold and you have some important exams coming up. If you catch this cold now, you'll have a very hard time in those exams. Let's not kiss until I get over this or until your exams are finished."

So, even though Margie has a strong desire to kiss you, she holds off her desire for the good of the two of you. That really is love. It may have the same results as using plastic wrap over the lips, but it says something completely different.

Well, Natural Family Planning is like choosing not to kiss. A couple chooses not to have marital relations during the time that

82

A Loving Non-Kiss

they know they are fertile. It means a sacrifice, but it also engenders greater communication and respect for each other's body and sexuality.

Margie: Father, you're comparing fertility to a cold, as if it were a disease?

Father JP: Actually, it's contraception that treats fertility as a disease. It looks upon fertility as an evil, something to be eliminated or destroyed.

Natural Family Planning respects the woman's fertility. It acknowledges that fertility is part of her feminine "I," part of who she is as a woman. Contraception, on the other hand, rejects this aspect of her feminine character. Contraception says, "I love you — everything but your feminine fertility."

Margie: But if a man is totally respectful and accepting of the fertility of his wife, then how can he accept using Natural Family Planning?

Father JP: That's a very astute point, Margie. But, we also have to remember that the cyclic nature of fertility is also part of a woman's feminine "I." A woman is not pure fertility, a baby-producing machine. There are many other important aspects of her feminine character. For example, her womanly attractive-ness and the way a woman shows affection draws men out of themselves, moving them to be generous.

Thus, the cyclic nature of a woman's fertility shows us that there is more to sexual intercourse than producing babies. It also shows us that God has designed it as an intimate expression of total self-giving, as well as a motor to help draw men and women to get out of themselves and give themselves to each other with greater generosity.

Margie: So if I were sick, it would be more respectful to Sam to refrain from kissing, rather than using plastic wrap to avoid spreading my germs. In other words, a kiss is more than just the nice feelings we get from the contact of each other's lips.

Father JP: Correct. The act of kissing includes a certain physical vulnerability. The act of not kissing respects that vulnerability in a charitable way, that is, without imposing one's own desires onto the other person's vulnerability. A kiss is meant to unite the two into one body (although not completely). When two people kiss, they accept each other as a person, including accepting each other's vulnerability.

Your having a cold is a temporary condition that makes Sam more vulnerable than normal. Choosing not to kiss respects him and the nature of the kiss, especially when this is motivated by charity and the good of the two of you.

Margie: I think I get it, Father JP.

Sam: Well, it doesn't convince me. Besides, all this doesn't make any difference, because the rhythm method doesn't really work.

Father JP: There are several methods developed in the last fifty years that are much more scientific than the so-called "rhythm method." These newer methods are the fruit of detailed scientific studies into the physical manifestations that accompany a woman's fertility. These methods are even more effective than most contraceptives. The latest study I have read found the NFP-Creighton Method 99.5 percent effective when properly taught and used.[9] The same study reported that oral contraceptives were only 97.0 percent effective. Even sterilization has a .2 percent failure rate! So, you see, Natural Family Planning can work. But the important thing is not so much the effectiveness of the method but what a person says by using it. Periodic abstinence preserves the integrity and the sacred meaning of the sexual union, whereas contraception and sterilization do not.

Another way to look at artificial birth control is from the point of view of God's role versus the couple's role in procreation. When the married couple comes together to form *one flesh,* they provide the physical conditions and the biological material for the engendering of a new human body. But God, too, has a role in the marital act. He not only unites the two spiritually, He provides for the spiritual conditions for new life.

Margie: You mean that it is God who creates the human soul.

Father JP: Yes. If God chooses, He creates a human soul, uniting the sperm and ovum to "produce" a human being at the moment of conception. Indeed the couple's love cooperates in this wonderful creative act, but it is God who transmits His own image and likeness to the new human being in each soul. It is similar to planting seeds in a garden: the man and woman cooperate in tilling the soil and planting the seeds, but it is up to God to give life to those seeds.

But a couple using contraception prevents this from happening; they prevent God from carrying out His role. They may say,

"We want the pleasures of sex but not the children." In such an act, what place is left for God?

Margie: None.

Father JP: Correct. God finds no business being there because the couple is not leaving any room for Him to create a new human.

Sam: So you're saying that contraception takes God out of the sexual act. But so does abstaining from sex altogether, since God cannot create a human soul there either.

Father JP: If by using contraceptives we exclude God from the male-female union then it means we also take love out of that union, because "God is love." So without openness to life, there is no openness to true love. Although the emotional aspects of love — the affection, infatuation, and attraction — may indeed be present, the spiritual element, which is essential to love, is eliminated because God is excluded from the act.

The abstinence of Natural Family Planning respects the God-given nature and *language* of the sexual act as a total, mutual gift of self. A couple abstaining from marital intimacy can show their affection for each other in other ways, such as kissing and hugging, and God is present in these amorous acts.

Sam: But, JP, God is all-powerful. He can create a child even when a couple uses contraceptives.

Father JP: True. There is no doubt that God is all-powerful; not even the laws of nature limit His power. However, God generally respects the laws of nature. For example, God could stop a bullet shot from a murderer's gun, but He doesn't normally do so. This does not mean He desires this evil, but He permits it in willing man's freedom. Likewise, God permits the evil of contraception even though it goes against His plan for love and life.

Even so, God sometimes does create a new human being when a couple uses contraceptives, since all artificial forms of birth control have failure rates. Even sterilization fails: God has designed the body to repair itself when we try to thwart His plans.

Sam: JP, doesn't Natural Family Planning also take your God out of the sexual act? It seems to be saying the same thing: "I want to be together with my wife, but no more kids, PLEASE!"

Father JP: Natural Family Planning tells God, "Please, no more kids, at least at this point in our lives. But we will respect Your plan. We will respect the *language* You have given to sex."

Margie: You mean, Natural Family Planning respects God's plan for the sexual act?

Father JP: Yes, Natural Family Planning respects God's plan for the sexual union as well as His plans for the family since it leaves the sexual act open to life, to God's potential life-giving work. It also respects the expression of total self-giving, the whole woman with her fertility and the whole man with his prolificacy.

Sam: But, JP, a friend of mine adopted a child a few years ago. During the process of adopting he and his wife saw some of the saddest and most neglected children. Hundreds of babies are born deformed or chemically dependent because their mothers were on drugs. Many women have children but are not mentally or emotionally able to take care of them. This leads to children living in an abusive environment or being taken away by a governmental child protection agency. Many go from foster family to foster family. Do you really believe that God wants unfit and emotionally unhealthy women to have children? Do you believe that God desires for crack babies to be born?

Father JP: Sam, you have brought up perhaps the most difficult question to our faith: the problem of evil and man's freedom. God creates man free and in doing so chooses to limit His own power by respecting that freedom.

It is important to distinguish what God wills from what God allows. God wills our freedom but in so doing, He opens up the possibility of our abusing that freedom with our sinful actions, even though He does not want sin. But not to allow the possibility of our sinfulness would negate our freedom.

It is God's will that a couple would make a commitment of faithful love to each other. However, He knows and allows the possibility of one or the other party to break that commitment, separating from his or her spouse and children, and to seek a relationship elsewhere. God does not will the mess produced by the selfishness of individuals, but He allows it by granting them their freedom.

God wills that new life would come into the world as the result of total and complete love of the parents of that new life, in the very expression of that love. God does not will that children be born out of an act of selfishness or pride, but in granting us freedom He also permits that some horrible things happen because of our abuse. If God did not will the child coming into this world, then that child would never have existed.

Sam, I could propose many other similar dilemmas. For instance, do you really think that God wants a child to come into this world who will be sexually abused by her father when she is ten or eleven years old, knowing that she may likely be emotionally disturbed, messing up the rest of her life? God does not want it, but He still allows it and calls us to try to remedy such situations. There are generous couples who willingly adopt crack babies or children with mental and physical handicaps. This is God's will and desire. Isn't this what the two of you are doing with disabled children?

Sam: Yes. We both work as volunteers with disabled children.

Margie: In fact, that is where we met. Although many of the children have severe disabilities, it is so moving to see how they respond to a little love and affection. And Sam is so good with those children. That is one of the reasons I was attracted to him.

Father JP: Well, I admire the two of you for hearing God's call to respond to the needs of those wonderful children.

God calls us all to help others, to go beyond our comfort zone and extend a hand to those in need. Perhaps we can use our talents to change the world so as to prevent unjust crimes to innocent victims from ever occurring. Or perhaps we can employ our science, technology, and personal sacrifice to heal and prevent diseases or birth defects.

But in all this we must use moral means to do so. We cannot just kill the father the day his daughter is born because we have a pretty good hunch that he is perverted and will abuse his daughter ten or eleven years down the road. That is not the right or moral way of dealing with the situation. If we have such a hunch, we have to help the father gain control of his passions and make sure — as best we can — that he is never in a situation where abuse could take place.

Sam: Still, JP, we are living in an age of science where we can manipulate the human body with medicine to do many good things that were not possible a few years ago. We could say, "Well, God designed the body in such a way that it gets cancer, so we should just leave it alone and let the cancer take its course." But we don't do that. In both contraception and Natural Family Planning, we use our scientific knowledge to prevent conception.

What if a couple just wants to have sex more often than Natural Family Planning allows? You tell them to respect God's design for the body — that fertility is part of this whole expression of love — but then you tell them to go ahead and take this medicine or get that operation to rid themselves of the cancer. You and Catholic teachings aren't consistent.

Father JP: Fertility and pregnancy are not diseases! You are the fruit of your mother's fertility and pregnancy as I am of mine. These processes are natural to a woman's body, by them new human beings come into existence. If we do not respect these processes, we don't respect the woman in her cyclic fertility. When we try to manipulate and control these processes at the core of a woman's being, we manipulate the very core of her feminine self.

Contraception is much different from taking medication or being operated on to rid oneself of disease. Contraception treats fertility as a disease to be extirpated, while Natural Family Planning treats fertility with respect and as natural to the feminine body.

Contraception is a deliberate act to prevent the conception and birth of a new human being. It is used simply to allow the couple to enjoy the pleasures of the sexual union. In Natural Family Planning, one chooses *not* to act, *not* to engage in sex during a period of time when the woman is fertile, to *forgo* certain pleasures for the good of the other and of the family.

Although medical research shows that the effectiveness of Natural Family Planning is similar to or better than most other means of birth control, God could still allow a child to be conceived, despite the couple's good intentions for using the Natural Family Planning. God is not deliberately excluded from that act.

Moreover, many forms of contraception have primary or secondary abortive effects. The IUD prevents the fertilized ovum — a tiny new human being in its early embryonic stage — from implanting itself in the uterine wall. The woman's child dies because it cannot get access to nourishment that it would receive from her uterus. The primary effect of the pill is to prevent ovulation, but since it cannot do so completely, it usually contains a drug that prevents implantation of any embryo conceived just like the IUD. Thus, birth control pills cause a mixture of temporary sterilization and micro-abortions. This is not to mention how many couples use full-fledged abortion as a backup when their birth control efforts fail altogether, which does happen. None of this is found in Natural Family Planning.

Is Natural Family Planning Ever Sinful?

Margie: I see the difference. Clearly Natural Family Planning is much better than contraception. But, is it ever sinful for a couple to practice Natural Family Planning? I thought I heard someplace that it was.

90

Father JP: It certainly can be. Natural Family Planning should be done for love, love for God and love for one's family and spouse. But if it were done for selfish purposes, it would be a sin.

It is possible to use Natural Family Planning with a selfish contraceptive attitude, for example, when the couple is not open to God's gift. Perhaps they choose to avoid having another child to afford a fancier car or a nicer home; that would be selfish. Perhaps they don't want the hassle of caring for another child, having to be tied down or not being able to enjoy life — fancy vacations, travel, etc. — that would be selfish too.

However, if they have serious reasons that make having a child right now unwise or imprudent, then Natural Family Planning may be the unselfish thing to do. Perhaps it is for medical reasons, because having another child would pose a health hazard for the mother. Or perhaps having another child would put undue stress on the husband, whose work or family stress could be bringing him close to a nervous breakdown. There could be many other reasons. Thus, love for God moves them to respect His established design for the marital expression of love; love for the family and one's spouse moves one to avoid what would objectively constitute a strain on that love.

But each couple must learn to discern whether their reasons for using Natural Family Planning are selfish or not. One of the best ways to discern this is through some spiritual direction or confession with a priest. The priest cannot decide that for them; that is their responsibility, not his. The priest is there not to make decisions for them, but he can help them make sure they are not missing anything important in making their decision. He can also help them to make sure they are seeking God's will and not just rationalizing their own selfishness.

Sam: I have heard that many priests just let couples make their own decision about birth control, yet you and the Pope are so insistent about birth control being wrong.

Father JP: I know some priests have a hard time with this teaching, but not because they refuse to accept the Church's Magisterium; most just don't understand it and don't know how to explain it well. A couple may come to a priest with a very difficult moral dilemma. Yet if the priest can't satisfactorily explain why they must stop using artificial birth control and live according to the Church's teaching, then it is just easier to say, "You must make up your own mind on this." Nevertheless, the Church asks priests to teach this doctrine clearly, without fearing that some may reject it.

In my experience as a priest, I am surprised how the vast majority of people respond well to this teaching. It really reflects the positive meaning of the whole teaching on human sexuality that we have been discussing.

Sam: JP, if a couple just decides that they have had enough kids already, is sterilization a valid option for Catholics?

Father JP: Again, Sam, this really isn't a "Catholic" issue at all. Prior to the Anglican Lambeth Conference in 1930, all Protestants held that sterilization and contraception were immoral, and Muslims still do. Gandhi was also opposed to birth control.[10]

Since our bodies are gifts from God, then what we do with our bodies affects our relationship with Him. Suppose you were younger, a senior in high school, and your parents decided to give you a very nice new car for your graduation gift. The only condition they put on it was that you had to pay for the insurance, gas, and upkeep of the car yourself. The car would remain in the garage until you got a job and earned enough to take care of those things.

How do you think they would react if, since you still couldn't afford the insurance, you would just go to sit in the car in the garage and listen to the radio or the stereo, perhaps dreaming of what it would be like driving down the highway?

Sam: I don't think they would mind at all. I would be fulfilling the conditions they gave me.

Father JP: Not only would they not mind, they would probably be happy that you appreciated their gift and that you were being responsible and respecting their conditions on their gift.

You did what with our gift!?

But what if you thought, "I don't feel like earning a living. I'd rather just live at home as long as possible, so forget about driving this car." So your friend offers you a thousand dollars for the car's engine and you let him remove it from the car. You can still go sit in the car to listen to the stereo, since you don't need the engine to do that.

How would that affect your parents?

Sam: They'd be very upset, but I guess they couldn't do anything about it since it was my car.

Father JP: You're right. Yet it would be very upsetting to see how you treated the gift they gave you. Saving and admiring the gift for a moment when you are capable of using it is pleasing to the giver; mutilating and rendering the gift useless offends the giver.

Sam: JP, but if we take this analogy to refer to sex between a couple — as you seem to be alluding to — then it seems OK to "listen to the stereo," that is, to enjoy the pleasures of owning a car without actually using it for its designed purpose.

Father JP: This is only an analogy to show how sterilization affects our relationship with God. No analogy is perfect. We have seen how God designed human sexuality to express a total, life-time commitment of the mutual gift of self as well as for having children. Perhaps we could compare "listening to the stereo" to an appropriate kiss, hug, or holding hands; certainly it is not on the same level of physical intimacy.

Sterilization of a woman is a rejection of her feminine character. Sometimes a woman even chooses this for herself, but in doing so it often is done with an underlying disdain for herself and this aspect of who she is as a woman. Such a woman rejects further motherhood because she hates the burden that it entails. She sees her fertility as a ball and chain, enslaving her to seemingly endless pain and suffering. This may be a sign that she even hates herself as a woman. But a woman's feminine character and fertility is a great gift for herself and the world, a key aspect of her gift of feminine genius.

Sam: Is this also true for men, JP?

Father JP: In a sense, yes, and in a sense, no. When a man is sterilized, sexual intimacies become strictly a manner of performance. Can I do "it" in a way that gives my wife pleasure? Can I do "it" in such a way that I get pleasure from it? It ceases to be an act that is connected with fatherhood. Male sterilization, then, is a rejection of paternity and more radically links his male identity to his performance.

Sam: But then if a married couple reserves sex for the woman's infertile periods, can they substitute intercourse with other sexual acts?

Father JP: The married couple is quite free to express their love and affection within marriage. It is true that couples using Natural Family Planning often develop many other ways to show their affection outside marital intimacy precisely for those moments when they must respect the woman's fertility. Consequently many married women who replace contraception with Natural Family Planning say they don't feel "used" by their husbands as they had before.

But there are limits to what couples should do. Alternative signs of affection ought not be done for mere selfish gratification, but truly be acts of self-giving as the sexual union ought to be. Not that pleasure is bad — in fact, it is created by God and quite good. But we human beings can use good things for self-centered purposes. A married couple practicing Natural Family Planning can express their affection in many ways, but it would be wrong for them to mimic intercourse in such a way so as to produce sexual pleasures without the possibility for conception. That would be equivalent to mutual masturbation, selfishly using each other for sexual pleasure without being open to new life and without the true and natural expression of the mutual and total gift of self.

Margie: What if the couple carried out the sexual act naturally but stopped just before any transmission of semen?

Father JP: This too would selfishly separate the sexual pleasure from the completion of the marital act and its consequences. Actually God addressed this case in the Bible and condemned Onan for it. God "slew" him; he took Onan's life to show us that this is a mortal sin.

Let's open the Bible to Genesis and read the passage. Here we go:

> But Er, Judah's first-born, was wicked in the sight of the Lord; and the Lord slew him. Then Judah said to Onan, "Go in to your brother's wife, and perform the duty of a brother-in-law to her, and raise up offspring for your brother." But Onan knew that the offspring would not be his; so when he went in to his brother's wife he spilled the semen on the ground, lest he should give offspring to his brother. And what he did was displeasing in the sight of the Lord, and he slew him also. (Genesis 38:7–10)

Sam: Everyone knows that God killed Onan not because he practiced birth control, but because he did not fulfill his legal obligation to marry his brother's wife. I think you got this interpretation wrong, JP.

Father JP: Prior to the modern acceptance of contraception, practically all Jewish and Christian theologians and Scripture commentators agreed that God slew Onan for "spilling the semen" and not for refusing to marry his brother's wife. The sentence for not taking one's dead brother's wife was much lighter penalty than the death sentence, as the Bible describes:

> *And if the man does not wish to take his brother's wife, then his brother's wife shall go up to the gate to the elders, and say, "My husband's brother refuses to perpetuate his brother's name in Israel; he will not perform the duty of a husband's brother to me." Then the elders of his city shall call him, and speak to him: and if he persists, saying, "I do not wish to take her," then his brother's wife shall go up to him in the presence of the elders, and pull his sandal off his foot, and spit in his face; and she shall answer and say, "So shall it be done to the man who does not build up his brother's house." And the name of his house shall be called in Israel, The house of him that had his sandal pulled off.* (Deuteronomy 25:7–10)

That modern interpretation that you were told doesn't seem consistent with this passage of Scripture.

Margie: So what limits does the Church place on what married couples can do?

Father JP: Look, the Catholic Church has a great respect for sexuality and for the freedom married couples enjoy. The Church does not wish to produce a detailed list of things that a couple can and cannot do. A couple should not be afraid about falling into sin every time they express their mutual affection. However, a married couple should keep two things in mind when expressing their mutual love and affection.

First, each one should have a great respect for the other as person, not using the other as an object for selfishness and self-gratification, but giving oneself to the point of self-sacrifice. The pleasure itself is not bad but can and should be enjoyed. It is the selfish pursuit of that pleasure that makes an act bad.

96

Second, the couple should respect the sacredness of the marital act itself, that is, they should respect sex's life-giving potential and its meaning in expressing the mutual and total gift of self. If a couple respects these two principles, they should not worry about offending God in this area.

Sam: JP, I follow your arguments, but I find it hard to condemn 98 percent of the world for using contraception. Even most Catholics seem to disagree with you on this.

Father JP: Sam, morality is not determined by public vote or approval. If that were the case, then God had no right for getting mad at the Jews in the Hebrew Scriptures when they melted down their jewelry and formed idols while Moses was on the mountain praying (Exodus 32). We could say the same about the election of Hitler and the Holocaust. Majority vote and approval doesn't make something right.

Margie: I'm sure that Sam and I agree with you there.

Father JP: And what if our society decided one day to accept rape, child abuse, or pedophilia as acceptable activity, would that make it moral?

Sam: No, of course not. Certainly what Hitler did was evil, whether or not the people approved of it. Actions that are clearly harmful to innocent people are wrong. But there are some moral issues that are not so clear, especially when done privately by ordinary people. That's what concerns me.

Father JP: Sam, I can appreciate your concern. We are proposing a completely different way of thinking.

Cloning and Test-Tube Babies

Sam: JP, although much of this way of thinking is attractive, something about it just doesn't seem right. For example, it seems to be biased against technology. Not only is the Catholic Church against contraception, I've also read that it opposes human cloning and test-tube babies. What do you make of this?

Father JP: Do you really think it is OK to create human beings for experimentation or use them as factories to harvest organs?

Sam: No. But much depends on how you define the human being. If we define a human being as a zygote formed at conception by the united egg and sperm, with God creating its soul, then cloning shouldn't be a problem. The entity formed by cloning isn't a human being, since cloning takes cellular material of an already existing human being and inserts it into an ovum whose genetic material has been removed. Cloning takes only the genetic material of a human being and stimulates it to grow independently. Since the soul cannot be cloned or split, then the entity formed — if it can be brought to "birth" — is not a human being, but just some biological or mechanical *thing*.

Father JP: Sam, your analysis is based on viewing human life in a purely mechanistic way. Certainly we know that human life does begin at conception from the union of sperm and ova. However, this does not *define* human life.

What is unique to human life is its personal subjectivity, which gives the person the capacity to pronounce an "I," to be the subject of an activity that he can call his own. A person has moral responsibility. The Church teaches that personal subjectivity is intimately linked to the physical body; one cannot separate the two, except artificially in the mind. In other words, the zygote would be human because it has personal subjectivity linked to its physical body.

Now if there ever is a human clone, and if it ends up having personal subjectivity, then there will be no doubt that it is a human being, and therefore it will have all the rights and responsibilities of a human being. Ironically its first fundamental right — to be born from an act of love between its mother and father — has been severely violated: it will be the product of "technological rape"!

Sam: But a fertilized ovum or zygote doesn't have any recognizable consciousness, it can't pronounce an "I" or any other word. Can't we treat it as we would any other clump of human cells?

Father JP: But when you are asleep, you don't have any *recognizable* personal subjectivity either. You cannot pronounce an "I" or exercise your free will. Nevertheless, you still retain all your dignity and human rights as a person. No one has a right to kill you, remove an organ from you, or experiment with your body just because you are not conscious. Unconsciousness or sleep doesn't cause a person to relinquish his human dignity or rights.

So no matter *how* the human body is physically *made,* the human being is a unique creation with a priceless dignity. Part of a person's dignity that he not be a mere product of human will and technological manipulation.

Margie: Father JP, many couples suffer a lot because they are not able to have children. I think that if science and medicine can help relieve human suffering to some degree it ought to be allowed. So if couples cannot conceive children naturally, why doesn't the Church allow them to use science to overcome their physical limitations?

Father JP: I agree that we ought to promote scientific research that will help alleviate human suffering, including infertility. Couples who discover that they are infertile do suffer greatly. That is why the Catholic Church actually encourages research with that aim, as long as it is done in a way that respects the sacredness of human life and the relational significance of the sexual act as sacred.

Much can and has been done to improve fertility in couples. Among other things, couples can increase their chances of conceiving a child by reducing or eliminating their consumption of alcohol, tobacco, and caffeine. Proper nutrition and exercise can also help, as well as avoiding saunas and hot tubs.

Science and medicine have developed techniques to improve fertility too. For men, drugs have been developed to increase sperm production and vitality. Surgery can reduce varicoceles (a form of varicose veins in the genitals). For women, the ovaries can be stimulated to produce more ova; fallopian tubes can be expanded, and progesterone augmented to increase fertilization and implantation. The Church allows and encourages this kind of research and therapy.

Sam: Then why is the Church set against having test-tube babies?

Father JP: In vitro fertilization — "test-tube babies," as you say — separates the act of love between spouses and the engendering of new life. For in vitro fertilization, the semen and the ova must be extracted from the bodies of the prospective parents and mixed together in a petri dish or test tube. Often the technicians gather several dozen eggs from the woman and fertilize them with the man's semen in a batch. They then freeze the zygotes — the fertilized eggs — until they can be implanted in the woman's uterus. When they do, they implant five or six zygotes in the woman's uterus, hoping at least one will implant fully and begin to develop. If more than one successfully implants itself in the woman's uterus, they will abort the "excess" zygotes. If none successfully implant, then they thaw out a few more zygotes and try again.

Notice how to produce one child, dozens of children have to die. How many children are now frozen in suspended animation with no parents to love them, doomed to a sad and uncertain future?

Sam: But what if the couple insisted with the doctors that they just fertilize one egg at a time, would that still be wrong?

Father JP: This is not just a problem of using the right technique. Just as it is wrong to remove fertility from the sexual union, it is wrong to remove the spiritual and sexual union from fertility and the engendering of new life.

In all this, the child becomes an object of production and not the fruit of human love. Every child has a right to be born as the fruit of love — as the fruit of love between his mother and father.

Couples who suffer from infertility and are unable to conceive often adopt children or volunteer to serve the needs of the Church, society, and families in need, and make a wonder-

100

TLC Laboratory:
We treat your future children with tender, loving care!

ful contribution. Their spiritual paternity is often rewarded many times more than their physical would have done.

Margie: But don't couples have the right to conceive a child of their own?

Father JP: Margie, nobody has a right to have a child. A child is a gift — a human person, not a piece of property. Some couples do treat their children like a pet or a piece of property, as though they owned the child. This kind of mentality arises from contraception and in vitro fertilization.[11]

The same is true for choosing the sex, the color of a baby's eyes or hair, or the like. You may have the right to choose the color of the carpet you purchase in your home, or the car you buy, but we cannot treat human beings like objects we own. Nor can we discard a human being if he or she is "defective." Try to think of this from the child's perspective. What would a child think if he or she were to discover that he was "designed" by his parents and that they wanted him just for his physical features? Is this not another form of child abuse?

Sam: JP, I don't know if I fully agree with all the things you're saying, but your logic is consistent.

Father JP: Sam, all I'd like to ask you to do is to think over the discussion we have had a little more.

Sam: OK, JP. I'll do that, but I won't promise you that I'll change my mind.

Margie: Father JP is not asking you to change your mind, Sam, he is asking us to think things over. Maybe you and I can think of other questions for him to answer. Perhaps that will help clarify matters for us.

Sam: You're right. I think we can do that. We'll see you next time, JP.

Father JP: Fair enough. I look forward to seeing you two soon.

Sex: For Bonding or Babies?

Sam puts off going back to see Father JP for some time. He often thinks about the conversations he and Margie had with him and wonders how worthwhile it would be to continue.

Then Sam learns that his younger sister has become pregnant out of wedlock. He's very upset, partly due to his disappointment with his sister, partly because of his anger toward her boyfriend who walked out on her after learning that he was a father, partly because of anger at Father JP and the Catholic Church for the teaching on birth control. All this motivates Sam to go see Father JP with Margie one more time, more than anything to vent his frustration.

Adoption vs. Single Parenting

Sam: JP, although I have calmed down quite a bit, I'm still angry and frustrated.

Margie: Father JP, Sam just found out last week that his nineteen-year-old sister is pregnant and decided to drop out of college to raise the child.

Sam: The guy she was dating dumped her as soon as he found out. My sister's life is never going to be the same. She will never realize her dream of becoming a doctor.

And this jerk she was dating, he is such a deadbeat. He doesn't even care about his own child.

(*Sam is practically in tears.*)

Father JP: You are upset, aren't you? How is your sister doing? Is she going to keep the child?

Sam: Yes, she is. No one in our family believes in abortion. She knows she is carrying a tiny child within her.

Father JP: You should be proud of her for that. Although she knows abortion is wrong, it still takes a lot of courage to do what she is doing.

Sam: Thank you, JP. Yes, she is quite a young woman. I just hate to see all that talent go to waste.

Father JP: Sam, it won't go to waste. If she does decide to raise the child herself, she is going to need every bit of her good heart and intelligence to raise the child well. It is particularly hard to do it alone. Has she thought about giving the child to a good family to adopt?

Sam: We have been trying to convince her that adoption is the best option, but she thinks she wants to keep the child herself.

Father JP: It takes even more courage for a woman to put her child up for adoption, but it probably is the best solution for the child. This solution guarantees that the child will have a good mother and father to give it the time and attention it needs to develop into a good, upright citizen, like you and Margie have. Also, this option would allow your sister and her boyfriend to get their own lives on track, to prepare themselves properly to take on the responsibility of being good parents. A child deserves to have two parents, and it really takes two parents to raise a child well.

I know it is emotionally very difficult to put one's child up for adoption, but I'll pray that she may have the courage to do what is best for the child.

Sam: Thank you, again, JP. I expected you to judge my sister more harshly. This wouldn't have happened if her boyfriend had used the proper protection.

Father JP: Why do you say that, Sam? Have they been discussing these concerns with the two of you? Normally using contraceptives or not is a pretty private issue.

Sam: No, JP, it's just that I know he's Catholic. My sister and I were musing over the fact that we were both dating Catholics. Of course, her boyfriend was not quite as serious about his faith as Margie is, but he definitely grew up in a Catholic family. And since the Catholic Church says "no" to contraception, what else would one expect to happen.

Father JP: Just because someone was raised Catholic doesn't mean he chooses to follow the Church's teachings. If he had, your sister would not have become pregnant since he would have waited until marriage. Also, abandoning his responsibilities to your sister and her child is not a Christian way of behaving either. So I doubt the Catholic teaching on birth control had much to do with what happened.

Why Is the Sexual Experience So Intense?

Sam: But if God really wanted us to wait for marriage to have sex, why did He make the sexual experience so intense? It seems that God almost wants us to sin. And I was also thinking about Natural Family Planning: if God wanted us to use that and not have sex so much, then He wouldn't have made it so intense.

Margie: Sam, don't you think God knows what He is doing? If the sexual urge weren't so strong, think of how few couples would be willing to have children, especially the men who tend to see children as burdens. The Original Sin of Adam and Eve has damaged our nature and made us weak. We're easily tempted and it's hard for us to control ourselves.

Father JP: Margie, although you make some good points, I do not think that procreation is the principal reason for God making the sexual experience so powerful.

Margie: Then what is the reason?

Father JP: Have you ever had a strong emotional experience, one that made a lasting impression on you? Perhaps you were in a serious accident, or nearly in one. Adrenaline would have poured into your bloodstream. The whole experience would have been etched into your psyche with little details triggering flashbacks. It could be smell of burnt rubber, seeing a car coming toward you, or hearing tires skidding. Then the adrenaline starts to flow again and you relive the whole experience.

Sam: Last summer I was hiking with some friends when I slipped and nearly fell off a steep cliff. It really scared me. Coming back down the trail a couple of days later, I froze when I neared that cliff. I simply couldn't move. That had never happened to me before.

Father JP: Why do you think that our human nature works this way? It's hard for us to remember everyday experiences or a few facts. So why can just one experience can leave such a powerful memory?

Margie: I don't know, Father, why?

Father JP: Because Nature wants us to avoid having too many life-threatening experiences, which could be hazardous to our health. Any sight, sound, or smell that is associated with a dangerous moment is etched into our psyche to trigger a warning and help us avoid those kinds of risky situations in the future.

Sam: What does that have to do with sex?

Father JP: Something similar is designed into the emotions attached to the sexual union.

Imagine that two people really love each other but decide to save sexual intimacy for marriage. On their wedding day, the bride goes down the church aisle in her beautiful white dress. She and the groom go before God, the Church, and before their family and friends, where they make that commitment to remain united to each other until the end of their lives. Afterward they have a wonderful reception where everyone has a marvelous

106

time — there is good food, good drinks, music, dancing, and the newlyweds are having the time of their lives celebrating the commitment they made to each other.

Finally the bride and groom come together for the first time on their wedding bed for a very intense emotional, sexual experience. The whole wedding, from beginning to end, and with all that is associated with it, is permanently etched into their psyche.

Later, when the honeymoon wears off and the couple goes through the inevitable harder times, the sexual experience will bring back the memory and reinforce the commitment that the two made on their wedding day. In fact, other things are psychologically associated with the wedding commitment by the sexual experience of their bridal bed. Perhaps seeing the type of flowers that were in the bridal bouquet; seeing people who were present at the wedding or the wedding pictures or dress; tasting a certain flavored cake. All these things can trigger a person to remember and relive that pivotal moment in their lives.

Margie: That makes a lot of sense. That's what I would want for my marriage.

Sam: But JP, wouldn't that psychological process also take place even if the couple has sex before marriage?

Father JP: The psychological process is quite different if the couple has sex before marriage. First, the sexual union is not linked to the commitment they made but to being together for an indefinite period of time. What does the wedding mean to such a couple? They have sex before they get married and they have sex after. There is very little difference in the way they live their lives between the before and after. The wedding was not much more than an excuse to have a party and take a special vacation trip — the honeymoon. That is why, when they hit upon more difficult times in their marriage, it is so easy to go back to the way they were before, to become unmarried again by divorce, because it was never such a big deal in the first place.

I remember it well!

Sexual intimacy complicates a dating relationship. Because of its bonding effect, it can get one or both individuals to become inappropriately attached to the other. Although one may temporarily experience the feeling of closeness and intimacy in sex, it also produces a long-term feeling of being physically "tied" to the other person, even after the relationship turns bad. This often leads to nasty and difficult breakups or, worse still, remaining in a relationship and even marrying the wrong person. Even if the relationship has long-term potential, sexual intimacies cause the couple to focus on their physical relationship instead of having fun and getting to know the other person.

There are also possible negative psychological consequences to having sex outside of marriage. For example, one man described his tormented situation: he led a very promiscuous life until he met a woman that wouldn't give in to his advances. He later realized his mistake and cleaned up his life. However, as he described the situation years after they were married, he has never been alone with his wife. Every time they start to become intimate, it triggers memories of past girlfriends and experiences. Although he does not want these thoughts, nor does he give in to them, they torment him, taking away from the "specialness" of the moment with his wife.

"Going All the Way" vs. "Doing Everything But..."

Sam: So you seem to be saying that as long as a couple does not go "all the way" their wedding will be more special and they will have a greater chance of having a lasting marriage?

Father JP: Well, Sam, certainly going "all the way" before marriage produces the type of intense emotional experience that engraves itself in our psyche and which takes away that special unique, bond-reinforcing experience of one's wedding night. But I am afraid I have to tell you that other types of sexual experiences do so as well.[12]

Oral sex acts, petting and fondling, passionate kissing and embracing can excite intense emotions similar to those aroused by sexual intercourse. This is why these are gravely sinful acts.

Margie: Are you saying that passionate kissing is a mortal sin?

Father JP: Remember, a mortal sin is one which destroys our relationship with God. Three conditions are necessary to commit a mortal sin: the action itself must be a serious offense against God and His commandments; second, the action must be done with full knowledge of its sinfulness; third, we have to deliberately consent to this action.

Although stealing is always wrong, stealing five dollars from our parents is usually not a serious matter; our parents wouldn't kick us out of the house for that. Stealing five thousand dollars would be different, a much more serious offense.

By definition, passionate kissing is kissing which arouses the passion in one or both individuals. We do not mean passionate in the sense of being intense — although intense kissing tends to arouse the passions. We mean passionate in the sense of arousing the passions for sexual intercourse. To deliberately arouse the passions or deliberately enjoy sensual pleasure outside of marriage is a serious offense against God and His commandments regarding marriage. It also is a way that one individual *uses* the other for his or her own selfish pleasure.

Now if kissing, or some other sign of affection, becomes passionate without our full awareness and consent — let's say because we are not expecting it to affect us or the other person that way — then it would not be a mortal sin. But it would become a mortal sin when we became aware of what was going on and we decided not to stop or do anything about it.

Sam: It seems a little extreme to me that God would consider kissing a serious offense.

Father JP: It is not kissing that is sinful but *passionate* kissing.

How would you feel about a man who got his enjoyment out of teasing a dog? This man would hold up a chunk of meat just out of the grasp of the dog, which would jump and try to grab the meat. The man would continue holding the meat out of its reach until the dog collapsed with exhaustion.

Sam: That would be cruel, but I don't think we could say that it is gravely evil.

Father JP: What if the man were doing it to your dog, how would you react?

Sam: I would go "ballistic."

Father JP: But, Sam, when we consider passionate kissing, we are not talking about a dog that belongs to God, but about a daughter or son for whom God has an immense love. Moreover, arousing the passions for sexual intercourse deals with the dignity of two human beings and the sacred expression of love

Boys will be boys... But that's my dog!

that is total and permanent. We are not just talking about arousing the appetite for feeding the stomach; we are talking about arousing and eliciting an act that is sacred, that belongs to a permanent commitment of marriage and which could possibly engender a new human being.

The most important thing to keep in mind is that your show of affection must respect each other as persons. Using another person as an object of pleasure or as a means for emotional security of *feeling loved* would imply treating that person as an object, not as a person.

Is Virginity Physical or Spiritual?

Margie: Father JP, how do these passionate acts affect virginity? Would you say that I have lost my virginity because I have engaged in passionate kissing and other passionate acts?

Father JP: What is virginity? What does it really take to be a virgin?

111

Sam: I have always understood that to be a virgin means one has not had sexual intercourse with another. This is why I think Margie feels a little nervous — because she still considers herself a virgin.

Father JP: The way you have defined virginity is kind of negative. If a woman told you that she was a virgin but would do all kinds of sexual acts, everything except intercourse (so she wouldn't get pregnant), would you think she was prepared for this wonderful and unique experience on her wedding night?

Sam: From what you seem to have been saying those past sexual experiences could very well continue to haunt this woman, so that she cannot feel alone with her new husband. On the other hand, perhaps she has lost her sensitivity such that those experiences no longer bother her.

Margie: I know some women who are so jaded that they don't have much of a conscience left.

Father JP: What about the man who does pornography and who undresses every pretty woman he sees in his mind? Do you think he is ready to establish a unique and lasting bond with his fiancée?

Margie: I certainly wouldn't want to marry a guy in a state of mind like that.

Father JP: Let's look at this issue from another angle, for instance, a woman who was raped as a child. Do you think she could be healed and have a decent marriage?

Sam: I would hope so, since she wasn't responsible for that action.

Margie: But it may take some time and counseling, because the emotions associated with the violent act could indeed affect her relations with her future husband.

Father JP: You are precisely right. The point that I am getting at with all these questions is that virginity is not *just* the physical state of not having had sexual intercourse with the opposite sex. It is much more than that. It is something spiritual. It is a decision and disposition of one's whole self.

Sam: A decision? What kind of decision is that?

Father JP: The flesh is blind, meaning that, physically, our bodies are not oriented toward any particular person, but are drawn indifferently toward any and every individual of the opposite sex. Virginity is a decision to give oneself whole and exclusively to one person, to one's spouse. It is to reserve sexual contact and the passion associated with it for that expression of total self-giving and committed love.

Virginity is a complete orientation — both physical and spiritual — of one's person, an orientation of one's whole being toward the person with whom one seeks communion. If because of violence (like rape or incest) one loses one's physical integrity, this doesn't mean one's total being cannot be oriented or reoriented to one's ultimate love.

But on the other hand, if one freely chooses to give physical and psychological intimacy to a person who is not his ultimate partner, then he will have a divided heart. Or if he freely chooses to give physical and psychological intimacy to the person who will be one's ultimate partner but does so without the lifetime commitment and for the wrong motive, then he too will have a divided heart. The same is true with the person who has a wandering eye and imagination. None of these people is properly speaking a virgin because he cannot give his whole being — heart, imagination, body, mind — to the person with whom he chooses to live the rest of his life.

Margie: But shouldn't we be trying to develop a spiritual and emotional bond between the two of us before we marry or even consider marriage?

Father JP: Yes, but in appropriate ways — ways that respect each other as persons and which do not produce attachments that limit the freedom of one or the other. Mild emotions generate tender and gentle bonds of friendship, which is what is appropriate before marriage. Appropriate signs of affection create proper mild emotions. So would exchanging love letters, poems, having "our song," calling each other by personal nicknames, and so on.

There are many little things that couples do for each other that deepen bonds of friendship: the compliments, the flowers, the little surprise phone call just to say "I'm thinking of you." Remembering birthdays and anniversaries, keeping in mind big events in the life of the other such as an important interview or test — all these things are important because they show that you are constantly thinking of the other and that his or her life is intimately linked to your own.

Can One Recover One's Virginity?

Sam: It seems like you are saying that only virgins should get married and that there is no hope for the likes of Margie and me. Can one ever recover the "specialness" that two virgins would have on their wedding night?

Father JP: Certainly virgins have a great advantage for establishing a lasting and happy marriage. But it is possible to recover that kind of "specialness" of virginal self-giving by reorienting one's being toward a unique and total gift of self to the one's ultimate love.

Sam: But how do you do that? It seems impossible.

Father JP: What is impossible for man is possible with God (Luke 18:27).

The first step toward recovering virginity is to be convinced of its priceless value and then to seek it by doing whatever it takes to obtain it. Purity — virginal love — takes prayer and struggle.

It is especially important that one prays to God for the gift of virginal love. Have you ever read the story of Tobias and Sarah in the Hebrew Scriptures? There we have a great example of a couple using prayer to prepare themselves for a virginal self-giving on their wedding bed. Sarah, Tobias's bride, had been married seven times before, but each of her previous bridegrooms had died on their wedding night because they lusted over her. Tobias obeyed the angel Raphael's instruction by praying before coming together on their wedding bed. This was their prayer:

Blessed are you, God of our fathers, and blessed be your holy and glorious name forever. Let the heavens and all your creatures bless you. You made Adam and gave him Eve his wife as a helper and support. From them the race of mankind has sprung. You said, "It is not good that the man should be alone; let us make a helper for him like himself." And now, O Lord, I am not taking this sister of mine because of lust, but with sincerity. Grant that I may find mercy and may grow old together with her. (Tobit 8:5–7)

Margie: That is a nice prayer.

Father JP: Yes, it is. Tobias knew he needed a sincere heart, one that was not divided by selfishness and lust.

It is good for dating couples to pray together during their courtship. Many people think that religious practice is something that can wait until after they are married. They are afraid to rock the boat, afraid that the other person may not be so religious and not want to go ahead in the relationship. It would be much better to dig a foundation and build a relationship on solid ground than to begin building without knowing what kind of foundation one has.

Sam: Is that all one can do — pray?

Father JP: No, of course not. We said that virginity is a decision to freely orient one's whole being to the person to whom one will give oneself. This means a series of decisions: to purify one's heart, to purify one's imagination, and to purify the tendencies of one's bodily senses.

First, to purify the heart means to control one's thoughts and desires for other people. If you begin to think about a person in one's past or desire that person, it is important to react, to say no to those thoughts and desires, and to direct one's heart and mind to something else, or to your love. Little by little our heart learns that we are no longer interested in that person of the past. We can even "punish" ourselves — like a parent does a child — by denying ourselves something good, like not listening to music for a while or to sit up without leaning our back against the chair for the next hour or so. This way our heart associates an unpleasant moment with the thought and desire for that person in our past and will want to avoid it in the future.

Sam: Are you sure this really works?

Father JP: Yes, it does. Once the virginal orientation of one's heart is lost, it takes work to fight against our compulsions to recover that orientation, but it can be done — I know people who have. It just takes effort to purify the imagination and the senses.

If the imagination begins to fantasize, you have to react to it in the same way. Seeking pleasure in imagining possible relationships and actions disorients us from exclusive self-giving love. Besides wrestling control of our imagination and changing it to something positive, we may also want to chastise ourselves with an appropriate "punishment" here too.

Purifying the senses means to do the same with our eyes, ears, touch — that is, anything that arouses desires for sexual pleasure. We need to learn to deaden ourselves to these stimuli, so that when one goes into marriage, our body and spirit, our senses, imagination and heart are all oriented to that total self-giving. Uncontrolled stimuli tend to remind us and make us relive previous selfish experiences.

When a person submits himself to this kind of discipline in which he does not give in to such attractive stimuli, then little by little he recovers his "virginity," that singular orientation of his whole being. Thus, he is able to make his wedding night a real special experience. He won't associate the wedding night with previous affairs.

Margie: Father, I learned a lot here. I have to rethink some of the things I did in the past. I think I need a little purifying, as you said.

Father JP: The reality is, we all do. None of us is completely free of our past faults. We need to acknowledge our infidelity with God and do everything we can to repair the damage within ourselves and the damage done to others. For Catholics, we have the Sacrament of Confession to help us get right with God.

Sam: What about us Jews, JP? We don't have such a sacrament.

Father JP: In the Hebrew Scriptures, the Jewish people did have sin offerings. If a Jew committed a sin, he had to go to the priest, mention his sin and then offer the sacrifice prescribed by the Mosaic Law (Leviticus 4–6; Numbers 6–7). Although you no longer have those sacrifices, you and we can offer our own prayer and little sacrifices along with a contrite heart, which God will not despise (Psalm 51:17).

Practical Advice for Saving Sex for Marriage

Sam: OK, JP, that is nice in theory, but in the day-to-day relationship, it is hard to avoid becoming intimate physically. We have already had troubles with that. I don't see it getting any easier.

Father JP: You have a point, Sam. It is not enough just to have good intentions when you date; you also need to learn proper ways of showing affection and strive to work at them.

Sam, what do you think is the purpose of affection?

Sam: Well, it is to show Margie that I love her and that I care for her.

Father JP: Yes. In marriage, affection is part of the gift of self. It is shown in small ways as well as the complete gift of self that manifests that complete spiritual self-giving.

In dating, affection has a different purpose, so each person should keep that in mind as they give and receive affection from

117

the other. They should think, "What am I saying when I give a "yes" or a "no" to the advances of the other?"

Many people show signs of affection on a date, attaching little or no meaning to it. For example, they will give their date a kiss, even kiss passionately, without any desire to continue the relationship after this particular date. Is this what a kiss should mean or say?

Margie: No. A kiss should say, "I love you."

Father JP: A kiss should say that you are special to me, that I want this relationship to go further. At the same time, by stopping there, I am also saying that I do not have a complete commitment to you.

Affection in dating should encourage the other person to want to give of him- or herself more, to want to get to know you better, and to open up and reveal himself more completely. Affection does this by showing that you care, that this person is lovable and that you accept him just as he is.

If we are not careful, affection can be used to manipulate the other person, to get him or her to give us what we want. In a sense, it is like flattery, saying what the other person wants to hear just to get what we want.

Sam: So are you saying that even a couple that is engaged to be married can't do anything more than give each other a peck on the cheek — say like when I kiss my grandmother good-bye?

Father JP: Certainly a kiss between a man and a woman engaged to be married has more to say than a good-bye kiss of your grandmother. Their kiss may express the commitment they have to commit their whole lives to each other for life, which will occur sometime in the near future. But in doing so, they must express and respect the freedom that each has to back out of that engagement for whatever reason he or she may choose.

Therefore, a kiss between those engaged to be married may be more intense than a simple act of affection. However, it ought to avoid passion, which begins the physical and emotional bonding process that does not leave each person free.

118

Those engaged to be married can show greater affection but they need to respect each other until the full spiritual bond is made in marriage.

Sam: How do you keep those signs of affection from going beyond the limit? Sometimes you care so much for another person that you just can't seem to stop.

Father JP: Begin by preparing yourselves for dating with prayer. You can do this as you are getting cleaned up and dressed. Try conversing with God and asking Him for His guidance, that this date would be an opportunity to get to know the person you are dating better and that you not be led "into temptation." Maybe the two of you could pray for a few minutes together at the beginning of your date. God will help you see beyond the temptation and ascertain the real good of the other or how your selfishness may hurt the person you want to love. He will help you "fast-forward" the temptation to recognize your potential mistakes before they happen.

Also, it is important to avoid places and situations where you would find it difficult to control yourself. Sam, in the past when you have found that you have gone too far with a woman, where did you do it?

Can't we find a better place to talk?

Sam: Usually it was in my apartment or at her house. Other times, it just happened when we were parked in the car.

Father JP: That's it. You were alone. If you avoid being absolutely alone with your date, you won't have any problems. Never let a woman come to your house when you are alone. Never go to a woman's house when she is alone.

Sam: What about in the car?

Father JP: Driving in a car is not usually a problem, because you are not absolutely alone. You are passing cars on the road and people on the street. It is only when you park in some isolated spot that you are together alone. So, if you want to save yourselves for marriage, live by this rule: never be absolutely alone with someone of the opposite sex. If you are driving and stop the car, get out and go someplace where you won't be tempted.

Yet sometimes the person you are dating intimates that he wants to be alone with you. What should you do then?

Margie: I'd just say "no."

Father JP: But what if he says to you that he wants to be alone because he really wants to share some very sensitive and intimate thoughts and concerns. What would you say to him?

Margie: I'd still say "no."

Father JP: I hope you'd go about it in a little bit more romantic way than that. Perhaps you could say something like, "Gee, honey, if you really loved me, we could be in a crowded subway and the whole world would disappear and we'd be alone. Besides, it is much more romantic to go to that corner booth of our favorite café or to go for a walk in the park together." The main thing is that we have to be prepared to say "no" and have an alternative suggestion.

Sam: This seems a bit extreme and prudish. If my friends found out that I was afraid to be alone with Margie, they'd never stop laughing.

Finally, honey, we can be alone!

Father JP: These same people don't know how to keep themselves and their bodies intact for the person they love. You cannot let them control the way you live your life. Besides, you are not going to marry your friends. If you lose them over something like this then they are not true friends.

Really, this is not an issue of being afraid, but doing whatever it takes to keep the relationship pure and meaningful. You may not be afraid of seeing a pornographic movie, but you wouldn't think about going because you know how it would affect your relation with Margie. If you truly want to wait for marriage — to make it really a very special moment for the two of you — then you will have to use means like these.

Sam: I'll give it a try and I am sure Margie will too. But you know, JP, human nature is weak.

Father JP: Please do try. You will find it easier the more and more you work at it.

Margie: We will.

121

Sam: You know, JP, I think I would like to have my sister come join us in these discussions. I am sure she would also benefit from them, even though it's a little late. Would you mind, JP?

Father JP: No, not at all. If she were half as open as you are, it would be a delight. And it is not "too late," since we can always learn from our mistakes to make sense of our lives and to help others not fall into the same pothole as we did.

Sam: Thanks, JP. I will see if she'll join us next time.

When We Stumble

A couple of weeks go by. One day Father JP is surprised when Sam greets him in the confessional. He has accompanied Margie and wants to talk privately with Father JP.

Struggles with Self-Abuse

Sam: JP, I don't know how this works . . .

Father JP: Sam? What a surprise!

Sam: Well, I don't want to go to confession. I just came to ask you a question or two.

Father JP: Sam, you have to be Catholic to receive the Sacrament of Confession, but of course you can always come in to ask a question or to seek some advice.

Sam: You won't tell anybody about what I ask you, will you?

Father JP: Sam, the priest keeps things he hears in the confessional a secret. It is similar to a doctor-patient or lawyer-client relationship in which one trusts that the doctor or lawyer will keep everything confidential. In fact, he has a strict legal requirement to do so. The priest has a similar duty, because if he reveals the sin of a person who confesses to him, he is automatically excommunicated and prohibited from exercising his priestly ministry. Although this is not confession, this conversation is of a similar nature and completely confidential.

Sam: The last time we met, you talked to us about different ways of orienting ourselves for pure love. I want to know whether it is all right to relieve oneself by masturbation. I have heard many people say that there is nothing wrong with it, even that it is a healthy release of tension. What do you think?

Father JP: Sam, masturbation is no relief. This way of stimulating yourself causes you to associate the strong emotions associated with the sexual act with self-gratification. This act expresses complete self-sufficiency: I don't need anybody else for my fulfillment. I don't need to give myself to anyone else to be a complete individual. I exist for myself.

When a person abuses himself in this way, he may attain some apparent relief and gratification, but the body is not satisfied. It produces even more bodily fluids and asks for more. It often causes one to go into an ever-increasing cycle of sexual self-seeking.

Sam: You are right on that score; it happens now much more than it did a few years ago. I thought that it was just that I wasn't doing anything with Margie. But what about the doctors who say it's OK?

Father JP: Some doctors may say it's OK, but they are looking at it from a strict physiological perspective. They are not considering the ethical ramifications. Nevertheless, there are others — psychologists and psychiatrists — who say the contrary, that those who carry out self-abuse tend to be more self-absorbed and tend to exhibit more antisocial behavior.[13] The momentary "high" they experience from the act is often followed by an even deeper "low." Often it causes them to have a lower self-esteem and they have a higher rate of sexual abuse of others.

Sam: But, JP, isn't it better to masturbate than to have sex before marriage?

Father JP: Sam, if you want to do it right, to go into marriage really prepared, then self-abuse is not the way to go. I have seen both men and women married to wonderful spouses who continue to practice this bad habit after their marriage. Although they are ashamed and feel dirty about it, they just can't help themselves, or so they say.

How can we give ourselves completely to another person if we have no dominion or mastery over ourselves, over the passions and desires that well up within us? Just as it is important to control our eyes to have true love, so too we must control our other faculties.

Besides, it is also a good preparation for marriage, because there will be times when you must abstain (for example, due to illness or pregnancy). If you have developed little or no self-control, then outside temptations will be much harder to resist.

Sam: I didn't think about that. So how do I overcome this habit? Certainly it doesn't seem to bother me as much when I am busy and have little time for myself.

Father JP: Keeping busy helps us struggle but it doesn't eliminate the habit. The way to do that is by purifying your heart, imagination, and senses, as we spoke about last time. Don't get down on yourself if you do fail, but get back up again right away — maybe giving yourself a little "punishment" — and start over. With prayer, determination, and the desire to really give of yourself to that someone special, you can conquer this.

Also, continue your efforts to guard your eyes and imagination, avoiding unnecessarily exposing yourself to arousing movies and pictures. This is hard to do in this culture of ours, which is constantly bombarding us with a barrage of erotic images. But if we avoid stimulating our libido unnecessarily, we will find it easier and easier to master our body.

Moreover, as you get more and more control over your passions, you will feel a greater sense of freedom, "Yes, I can control myself. I am not weak. I cannot be manipulated in this way." It will also give you greater confidence to be able to conquer yourself in moments of temptations that may occur with women now, before you are married, and especially later when you are struggling to be faithful to the woman you love.

Sam: What about when you get in one of those depressed, kind of lonely moments? It's in moments like these when it becomes particularly hard to resist.

Father JP: That is certainly true. When we feel lonely, physically exhausted, sleep deprived, stressed out due to work or other issues, we are particularly weak in mind and body. It's Nature telling us that we need to take a break. It helps to anticipate these moments, make arrangements to get extra rest, to exercise (especially sports that involve others), and to spend more time with friends. All of this helps.

Pornography

Sam: Thank you, JP.

Before I leave, would you mind if I ask one last question? It's a bit theoretical, but it has been bugging me for awhile.

Father JP: No, I don't mind. What is your question?

Sam: In the use of nudity, how do you distinguish pornography from serious art? The distinction seems awfully subjective to me. Wouldn't it be easier to say that all nudity is bad?

Father JP: As I mentioned in one of our earlier meetings, nudity in art does not have to be immoral. But to be moral, it should not only convey the beauty of the human body, but also the dimension of the body as a very personal nuptial gift, a unique gift that is given to the one person to whom one has chosen to give one's whole self in marriage. Nudity signifies a deep sense of personal trust and complete self-donation to the other person who is conscious of that gift and responds to it with his or her own trust and donation. This interpersonal dimension of the male and female human body is a visible part of the structure of the human person. Art can and indeed should portray this in a respectful and dignified way.

Yet at the same time, art cannot help but "objectivize" the body. When portraying the human body, art must take a bodily figure of a real human person with all its interpersonal meaning and turn it into an anonymous object that can be viewed by an unlimited and undetermined set of spectators. In other words, in portraying the human body the artist must take into account how the spectator will react to his work, for example, the artist must consider the possibility that a spectator may use his representation of the human body as a means for selfish sexual gratification.

Sam: But isn't that the moral concern of the spectator, and not the artist? If the artist's intention is good, if his intention is to represent the beauty and dignity of human love, for instance, then why should he have to be concerned about how the spectator will misuse it?

Father JP: Perhaps it would help to look at the work of art as if it were the precious son or daughter of the artist, the cherished fruit of his creative love, since that is how many artists view their work.

With this is mind, are not good mothers and fathers concerned about how strangers view and treat their son or daughter?

Sam: Of course.

Father JP: Even when they give their daughter or son away in marriage, they want that daughter or son to be treated well, with love and respect by their new spouse.

A good artist has a similar concern. He does not want his precious creation to be "raped" or mistreated by anyone.

Sam: But wouldn't that eliminate nudity from art altogether?

Father JP: A mother and father cannot keep a son or daughter locked up in their house, which would be the only way to prevent any possibility of abuse. If an artist takes reasonable care that ordinary people would treat his work of art with respect, then he should not feel bad and at fault if some unsuspected and perverted soul abuses his work.

In contrast, the person interested in doing pornography is like a pimp who peddles prostitutes. This person is indeed interested

Excuse me, that's my daughter!

in having people use his women for selfish pleasure because this is how he makes his living. He is not interested in the beauty or dignity of the human body; he is not concerned with the interpersonal character and meaning of the body; he is just interested in profiting from sensual pleasure that may be produced from his work.

Sam: Although I get your analogy, JP, it seems a bit exaggerated because a piece of art is just an object and not a person.

Father JP: You're right, Sam, but at the same time an artistic representation of a human being is quite different from one representing a bowl of fruit. An objective depiction of a person is more serious. Saying "I hate asparagus" has a lot less gravity than saying "I hate my mother." The latter "objective" expression would have much more serious consequences on my relationship to my mother, father, brothers, and sisters than any comment about asparagus.

The interpersonal character and meaning of the body in its naked state is an important factor. If the "objectivized" human body inclines ordinary spectators to appropriate and abuse the anonymous body for selfish pleasure, it would be immoral. True art should respect the personal sensitivity and the sense of shame of the general public. Art should represent the human body in such a way as to preserve the truth of its whole meaning, the interior world of values and interpersonal communication associated with that body, especially in the naked state. If this is done, the viewer does not feel drawn to lust and sensual satisfaction, but to marvel at the truth, beauty, and mystery contained in the human body.

Sam: How would this differ from pornography? Many men and even some women consider photographs of nude women and men to be art.

Father JP: Pornography has no respect for the personal sensitivity and the sense of shame of the general public. It is designed to arouse, to produce sensual pleasure independent of the nuptial meaning of the human body. Our looking at another human being for the purpose of sensual pleasure transforms that person into an object with no respect for her personal dignity and value. And as we saw earlier, it has drastic effects on our relationships to other.

Sam: That kind of makes sense, although it doesn't fit into the current mind-set of our society.

Father JP: You're right, but hopefully more people will be concerned about these issues and do something about them. Besides, it doesn't matter what society thinks. You and I must do what is right.

Sam: Thanks again, JP.

Sam gets up to leave, but Father JP has a question for him.

Father JP: Sam, before you go, do you mind if I ask you a question about our previous meetings?

Sam: No problem.

Father JP: Well, you didn't seem convinced by my arguments against contraceptives. Was there anything missing in my reasoning?

Sam: You're right about my not being convinced. I didn't have any real objections to your logic. I just found it extremely difficult to accept. Like most people, I think I would also find it too big of a sacrifice for me to put into practice.

Father JP: Have you ever thought what you would do if you married Margie?

Sam: Yes, I've been thinking about that possibility.

Father JP: What would you do if the two of you were married and she insisted on not using contraception? Would you ask her to go against her religious convictions? Would you force it on her?

Sam: No way. I would never want to force her to do anything. That would be wrong.

Father JP: Then if you married Margie, would you be ready to do without contraception?

Sam: I don't know if I could. Perhaps I'd be the one who would use it and not bother her conscience with the matter.

Father JP: The Church's teaching applies to the joint act between the couple, not who's doing what to prevent conception. Each marital act must be open to life. So it would still go against her Faith.

Sam: I didn't realize that.

Father JP: That's why it is important to think these issues out beforehand and to work on that self-mastery. If you can better control your passions and direct them toward the good of your love and your family, then I think you will prove it to yourself that you can be in control. It may even help you to accept the logic of love regarding contraception.

Sam: Well, JP, you certainly have given me things to think about and to work on. I'll give it a try. And I do look forward to our next meeting.

Oh, by the way, I haven't been able to convince my sister to come join us, but I'll keep working at it.

Father JP: Please do, but respect her freedom. So long for now.

How Far Is Too Far?

Margie was right behind Sam. This time she wanted to talk to Father JP before the confession, to clarify some of her doubts about sins.

Margie: Father, this is Margie. Do you mind if I ask you a question before I do my confession? I really want to do it right.

Father JP: That's fine, Margie.

Margie: What I want to ask you, Father, is how far is too far in dating?

Father JP: The question you ask is somewhat negative. A better question to ask is, what should I do to make my date with Sam really special?

Margie: Yes, Father, you are right. But sometimes you just need to know what are the limits beyond which a Christian cannot go. My parents never really talked to us about this; I guess they just assumed we'd get it in our Catholic education. Our classes in Catholic school focused more on relationships. They had us taking care of a bag of flour as if it were a child to help us b⌐ ome aware of the responsibility of becoming a parent, but they never instructed us on what was proper and improper in dating. I guess they assumed we'd get the idea that we shouldn't get pregnant until we are ready to take on the responsibilities of a child. Isn't there any other criterion for dating?

Father JP: Well, Margie, there is. However, I like to try to avoid the tendency to reduce Christian morality to a list of minimums, or "don't do this" statements.

Margie: I can understand that, because sometimes we want to seek a little selfish pleasure and we want to go as far as we can, but that is not the right attitude. But don't you have any advice you can give to orient me in what is and is not proper in dating?

You're Married...to God...to Christ!

Father JP: Actually, the advice I like to give is pretty simple: always act as though you are married—married to someone else! For example, if you were married to someone else, how do you think your husband would feel if he discovered you passionately kissing Sam?

Margie: He would be livid! But I'm not married.

Father JP: Oh, yes you are! You are married to Christ. All Christians are, through our Baptism. St. Paul makes this clear in his letter to the Corinthians:

> I [Paul] feel a divine jealousy for you, for I betrothed you to Christ to present you as a pure bride to her one husband. (2 Corinthians 11:2)

So a Christian should behave as one who is married, not married to her boyfriend or to his girlfriend, but to Christ. How would Christ feel if you were to passionately kiss another man or do some other passionate act?

Margie: He'd be very disappointed and upset with me. But does that mean we shouldn't even kiss each other?

Father JP: Our society has made the kiss into a semisexual act, but it isn't. It is an act of affection as long as it doesn't become passionate, arousing the appetites for the marital act. Then it would go beyond affection.

You are my life forever!

Parents and children kiss each other and many married adults will give adult friends a kiss — even those of the opposite sex — as a greeting. A kiss of this kind is not offensive to one's spouse at all.

The bottom line is: always act in the way that your husband, Christ, would not be offended. You might say act in the same way the Blessed Virgin Mary and St. Joseph would have treated each other before and after they married.

Margie: But what about after a couple gets married? How would Christ feel then?

Father JP: When two Christians walk down the aisle and go before God, the priest, the Church, before his or her family and all society, and when they make that commitment to love, cherish, and serve the other until death do them part, then the groom becomes Christ for the bride and the bride for the groom. From that moment on, all marital acts become acts of love for Christ, as long as selfish lust is not the motive. Remember the prayer of Tobias?

Margie: Yes.

Father JP: Well, he declared his love sincere and free from lust. That is necessary for true marital love.

Margie: What about Sam? He's not Catholic, he's not even Christian. Should Jews follow the same criterion if they don't believe in Jesus Christ?

Father JP: God showed the Jews that they had a spousal relationship with Him. God chose the Jewish people like a young man chooses a woman to make a marital covenant (see Ezekiel 16 and 23; Hosea 2; Jeremiah 3; Isaiah 54). Certainly Christians have a more developed vision of this. In the fifth chapter of his letter to the Ephesians, St. Paul shows us how Christ's relationship to His Church is the model for the relationship between a man and woman in marriage.

But to answer your question, yes, Jews are called to follow the same criterion, to behave as one married to God.

Margie: Now may I go to confession? I unwittingly left out a few things in my previous confessions.

Father JP: If you did not deliberately leave them out, then those sins were already forgiven. But you are correct in bringing them before the Judge, to receive advice and to make sure your intentions are sincere.

Margie: Thank you, Father JP.

The Purpose of Dating

About a week later, Sam and Margie return. They have been discussing their relationship and have decided to save sex for marriage. However, embarrassingly they backslid a little bit and became more physical than they intended.

Having Fun Getting to Know Each Other

Margie: Father, Sam and I have been talking and we really do want to save ourselves for marriage. But, despite our good intentions, we find it hard. In fact, we fell into passionate kissing the other night, even though you helped us to see that it was wrong. Is there anything more we can do?

Sam: I've been working on that self-purification stuff that you suggested, but, as Margie said, I think it's going to be kind of tough to live out the ideal you suggested.

Father JP: First of all, the two of you are on the right track. You have the basic desire to do the right thing; I must commend you for that. But it is also important to use the right means and to learn how to date properly.

Sam: I guess that's what we are getting at. But I have to admit, I'm still a bit skeptical about whether this ideal is really possible.

Father JP: Perhaps we need to start with a basic question: what is the goal of dating? What should a couple seek to accomplish by dating one another?

Sam: Most of my friends date just to have fun.

Margie: But also they do it because they have an interest in falling in love. It's not just for fun; it's for companionship, to fill a basic desire to share oneself and be a part of someone else's life. We date in order not to remain alone.

Father JP: The most important reason for dating is to get to know whether or not the person to whom you are attracted is the type of person you want to marry. Certainly dating must be fun and it does fill a certain void in the heart. Yet you should only give your heart to the other little by little, as you get to know the person and clearly see him or her as compatible with you, someone whom you want to be permanently part of your life.

Margie: What kinds of things should a woman try to get to know about her boyfriend before giving him her heart?

Father JP: You should think long term. One thing is to get to know what the other person enjoys doing. The couples who focus on sex never learn what their partner enjoys. Then when they do get married and sex becomes a little routine, they don't know what to do to revitalize the romance.

Dating is a good opportunity to get to know what the other person likes and dislikes. You may find that the two of you enjoy walking on the beach or hiking in the mountains or bowling with friends. While dating you can compile various special moments doing things that you enjoy. Then when you are married and the kids come along and the pressures of life seem to consume you, you may want to "relive" one of those dating experiences. You may propose to your spouse to go for a walk along the beach at sunset, and without even trying, you will rekindle the spark and romance of a similar moment during the time you were dating.

Couples who focus primarily on the physical side of their relationship often have little or no experiences to fall back on when the marriage becomes harder or a little tedious.

Sam: Is that all there is to dating, getting to know what the other thinks is fun?

Good Marriage Preparation

Father JP: No, but it is significant. How do you think a couple would fare if the wife hated outdoor activities, whereas the husband loved and lived for camping, hiking, skiing, hunting and fishing?

Sam: It might be difficult.

Father JP: Yes, it might. It is not that it is impossible to adjust. The wife might find herself home alone from time to time as her husband goes on his hunting expeditions alone. Perhaps the husband will find that most of his hunting is done in the local shopping mall in order to appease his wife. One or both will have to make a significant sacrifice.

It is also good to spend time doing some activities that are mutually enriching, like going to an art museum, or the opera. This helps a couple to go beyond the physical and to see what spiritual and cultural values they share.

Margie: As we date, what other things would help us get to know each other better?

Father JP: Doing some social work together could be very beneficial, helping needy children for example. In this way you see how generous the other person is and how well they deal with needy people.

Sam: We already do that. In fact, that is how Margie and I met.

Father JP: That's great! You're both on the right track there.

I recall reading a story about a young man who had a severely handicapped and bedridden brother. One day he brought a young woman home to meet and have dinner with his family. Before the family ate, someone would first take some food up to the handicapped brother, who needed to be spoon-fed. The young man asked his date if she would like to join him as he went up to feed his little brother, but she declined. That was all he needed to tell that this woman was not for him.

Sometime later, the young man brought home another young woman that he was dating. And again, the issue of feeding his brother came up. This time, the young woman said yes, that she'd like to join him. In fact, after a few minutes watching her boyfriend spoon-feed his brother, she asked if she could take over and she finished the task joyfully. This time, he knew that he had a winner, someone worth marrying.

Margie: That's a neat story.

Father JP: The main thing I think it tells us is to think long term when dating. Don't think about instant gratification, but "How would I like to be treated as a husband or a wife? Would this person treat me that way? How would he treat our children?"

Margie: Sam treats me very well—most of the time.

Father JP: Of course he does; he wants to win over your heart. But will he continue to do so when that is no longer an issue?

Margie: I hope so.

Father JP: The best way to find out how a person would treat you in a long-term relationship is to see how he treats others with whom he already has a long-term relationship. For example, one should observe how a man treats his mother or how a woman treats her father. How do the brothers and sisters fare? How does he treat his friends and even his enemies? Sometimes that is how spouses treat each other, at least in difficult moments. The more you get to know about how the person you date treats people, the more you will know how you will be treated—at least there shouldn't be too many big surprises.

Sam: That makes sense, but you don't make any allowances for people changing. When you date someone, especially someone special like Margie, it really motivates you to exceed yourself and try to make yourself the type of person worthy of her love.

Father JP: You're right; people can choose to change. But we are creatures of habit. Old, ingrained habits that are part of who we are take much effort to overcome. One can never tell how long the motivating desire to love and be loved found in dating will last. In making life decisions, you have to take all the information into account. Dating ought to be a period of information gathering: getting to know yourself, what you look for an ' need in a spouse, and getting to know the other person. Then you should be able to answer these questions: "Are the two of us really compatible? Do I have what it takes to make this other person happy, even after the magic wears off? Does the other person have what it takes to make me happy?"

How Compatible Are We?

Margie: Father JP, what qualities should a woman look for in a man to be able to tell whether he is "Mr. Right"?

Father JP: Well, each person is different, but there is one criterion that I find works. When you look at someone as a potential spouse, ask, would I choose this man to be my father? Or would I choose this woman to be my mother?

A woman should look for a man who would be a good father, one who could provide for the family and who would be a good educator and disciplinarian of the children without being too harsh. If you would not choose this man for your father, then why would you force such a father on your own children? This is where you must begin.

A man should look for a woman who would be a good mother, one who loves being with and caring for children. A good mother has to be a good teacher and be able to deal with the little foibles of children, knowing when to come down hard on a child and when to overlook minor childish things. You should look for a woman who expresses affection for children as you think they would deserve and a woman who can manage a household, coordinate household chores and meals — although the man may take on these responsibilities in some families.

Sam: But just because a woman would be a good mother doesn't mean she'd be a good wife.

Father JP: Compatibility has many facets. Each person going into a marriage situation brings with him or her all kinds of untold expectations that can be a source of future conflict. One is often even unaware of one's own expectations. But there are ways to discover what are those unmentioned expectations that are potentials for disaster.

One way is to look to one's own family. If a man grows up in a family in which his mother was quite servile to his father — picking up after him, buying his clothes for him — then likely he will expect his wife to do the same for him. If his mother was a

Susie, I think he's a keeper!

good cook and prepared certain dishes that really appealed to him, then he will likely expect the same in his own family.

Likewise, a woman may have been raised in a family in which her father gave the children a lot of attention, took the family on camping trips, cared for the garden, and was at her mother's beck and call. Well, it should be of no surprise to either that she expects more or less the same from her future husband.

Sam: But a guy cannot be a clone of a woman's father, can he?

Father JP: No, of course not. However, these are the untold expectations. A person should look at both his own family and his or her potential spouse's family to get to know now what things could be problems later.

For example, if a guy is a mamma's boy, whose sense of his self-worth and identity comes from trying to please his mother — and she uses this to control him — then you know beforehand what life is going to be like. His mother will be in control long after he marries. If before the marriage a father is habitually negative and critical of a son or daughter, especially of their dating relationship, then likely he'll be critical and negative afterward. Or if a woman must get her mother's permission for every decision she makes, then she'll do the same after she gets married. It is so important to know the family dynamics beforehand so as to know what to expect.

When the two of them discuss these things, they can make the choice to accept the person the way he or she is with all the family baggage, and one can choose to adapt one's life to the other's way of being or not. One can also choose to change one's life, to work on some defect, in order to meet the expectations of the other, and it is good to make these little decisions and try to live them out long before letting the big decision become a lifetime commitment.

Sam: But can we wait until we get married to discuss these matters?

Father JP: Sam, to get married is a decision that will affect your life, the life of the person you marry, and the lives of your children. We can't play with people's lives.

This is what dating is all about: getting to know oneself and getting to know one's potential spouse, really getting acquainted, but hopefully much deeper than the typical relationship nowadays.

Have the two of you talked about each other's faults and weakness?

Sam: No, not really. But Margie's are so obvious and mine . . .

(*Sam said this in a joking manner, as he winked at Margie and she returned a smirk.*)

Father JP: Don't be afraid of being up front with each other about each other's faults and weakness. We don't change easily and we shouldn't expect the other person to change.

Ask yourselves, do I accept this person with his or her faults. Am I willing to live with this for the rest of my life? If not, then please don't even consider marriage.

Margie: All this is quite a bit more than Sam and I have gone over so far. I guess we have some work to do. Are there any other things we should discuss before making the decision to marry?

Father JP: A couple needs to discuss what is important to each other. They need to discuss their values, what things they will not compromise. This is much more important than discussing their likes, dislikes, and interests, although that is necessary too.

Unfortunately many fear discussing certain matters or revealing certain issues that they know may cause the other person to back out of the relationship. A person may intentionally or unintentionally deceive the other, again out of fear of rejection, painting a picture of himself which is humanly and morally more attractive than he really is. Worse yet, one can misinterpret the actions of the other as a sign of what the other believes instead of discussing the matter openly and forthrightly.

For example, there was a Catholic woman who was dating an agnostic man. The woman made it clear to her boyfriend that her faith was very important to her and that she would follow the Church's teaching. She refused his sexual advances for quite some time. But as the relationship got serious and the two talked marriage, she gave in to his advances, using artificial birth control in order not to get pregnant out of wedlock. After they were married, they continued using contraception for a time until the woman's conscience got the better of her. When she made the decision to stop using contraceptives, he really resented her decision. He said that she was a different woman than the one he had married and that he was contemplating ending the marriage. He knew about the Church's teaching concerning contraception before they married; he just assumed by her actions of giving in to premarital sex with contraception that she hadn't intended to follow this part of Church teaching.

So it is extremely important to be totally honest — in word and action — with the person you desire to marry. You want them to accept you as you really are and not some false caricature that you pretend to be. This may be hard, but each has to overcome his fears and manifest himself just as he is. This is absolutely necessary.

Should Religion Matter in Choosing a Spouse?

Margie: Father, what about religion? Should that be a factor in making this decision?

Father JP: Certainly. I was wondering if you were going to bring this up.

Differences in religious practice often cause tension in a family, even if one or the other doesn't practice or doesn't believe, or even when the two are of the same religion but one of them practices and the other doesn't. This tension can arise for various reasons. Perhaps the religious partner has certain hopes or expectations that the other may convert or change after they marry and have children. When this doesn't happen, then resentment builds and little things become much bigger. Another scenario is where the nonreligious person feels jealous of the other's love for God over and above him or her.

Other reasons for possible tension may be the religious upbringing of the children. If the religious party makes an effort to raise the children in his or her faith, the other party may resent that and feel that he or she is judged as not being "good" in the mind of the other spouse and children. Tension may also develop when one doesn't get reinforcement in the raising of the children in religion. Beyond feeling alone in this task, the religious half may even find his or her spouse undermining the religious teaching and moral values he or she is attempting to impart to the children.

These are the underlying pressures that make marriages of mixed religions difficult. It should surprise no one to discover that the divorce rate among such couples is higher than those composed of individuals of the same religion.[14] Frankly, mixed religion complicates family life. Children have do deal with issues like "Why doesn't Mommy or Daddy go to church with us?"

Sam: Does that mean that a couple from different faiths should never consider marriage? My mom is Jewish and my father is a nonpracticing Christian, but they seem to have done fairly well together. Although I may be a bit partial here, I also think they did a decent job raising my sister and me.

Margie: Sam, I think your parents did a great job.

Father JP: I do too.

I wouldn't say absolutely that a couple of differing religious belief shouldn't consider the possibility of marriage, but I would say that it is an important factor that they should take into account in making this life-orienting decision. One's faith is key to his or her personal identity. Such a couple then would have a very important area of their lives that they would be unable to share with each other. Also, the more religious party will be alone in the rearing of the children in his or her faith.

Again, I go back to the criterion I suggested earlier. As a woman, would you choose a man without your faith beliefs to be your father? As a man, would you choose a woman of a differing religion to be your mother? The answer is probably not. So why choose that for your children?

Sam: Why is this such a big deal? Can't couples learn to keep their religious beliefs and practices to themselves, and share everything else?

Father JP: I wouldn't recommend it. Religion is one of the deepest dimensions of our being, an intimate part of who we are as persons. It may not seem to be particularly important to you now, but you cannot detach yourself from it entirely. It would be like detaching yourself from your relationship to your mother and father — they are part of who you are.

Imagine a man and a woman of different religions marrying and having a family. Later the woman starts taking her religion much more seriously. The desire to share this deep and personal side of her grows with her faith, but her husband will have nothing to do with it, so she goes to church on her own. There

If I had know this before I married you...

she meets this attractive man with whom she finds an outlet for sharing all her deep and personal religious sentiments.

Sam: I hadn't thought of that.

Father JP: This is not an uncommon situation, especially with women.

Moreover, Sam, if you leave religion out of your dialogue with Margie, you'd be missing out on a great opportunity to develop a deeper union with her. The more you two share this deep and intimate dimension of your lives, the closer you will become.

Margie: Given that Sam and I come from different faith traditions, do you have any suggestions for us?

Father JP: First pray to God for the guidance to do His will and not your own. Love — or better said, infatuation — tends to blind us to reality, so you want the strength to make the right decision even though you may have a strong attraction to the other person.

Second, discuss your religious beliefs openly; don't hide your beliefs out of fear of rejection. It is much better to receive the rejection before marriage than after. Discuss what your expectations are: frequency of going to church, a yearly weekend retreat (if that is important to you), how much you pray, and how you would like to celebrate the holidays. You must also discuss how important it is to have the wedding in your own tradition. A Catholic is almost always required to marry in a Catholic church; if there is a serious reason not to do so, then the required dispensations must be sought. Catholics must also receive marriage preparation by the Catholic Church.

Third, discuss how you plan on raising the children. What expectations do you have from the other person for support in raising the children? In mixed religion marriages the Catholic must promise to "to do all in his or her power to have all the children baptized and brought up in the Catholic Church."[15] Although the non-Catholic is not required to make this commitment, it would be wrong for the Catholic party to hide this commitment from his or her fiancé or to exclude it from their commitment to each other.

Sam: Why not just let the children decide when they become of age? It seems somewhat presumptuous and overbearing for the Catholic Church to insist on the children being raised in its beliefs.

Father JP: Certainly that may seem to be the case. However, the Church sees the children of her children to be her own. The Church feels responsible to look after them and wants them to have all the means to grow spiritually.

What would you think of a married couple if they decided not to teach their children any morality and to let the children decide for themselves what is right or wrong?

Margie: That would be horrible. They would be creating little monsters.

Sam: You don't seem to be giving much hope for couples like Margie and me.

Father JP: You two are exploring a decision that will have a profound effect on the rest of your lives, on your future happiness, as well as on the happiness of the children you bring into the world. The Church has a lot of experience in this area and doesn't want you or anyone else to be unhappy or go through unnecessary turmoil. You really have to think out the consequences of your decision before you make the leap.

Sam: Does the Church ever require the non-Catholic party to convert?

Father JP: No. The Church would never force anyone to convert, especially against his or her conscience. Faith is a sacred and free act and must be guarded as such. However, we would encourage that party to learn more about the Catholic Church. One reason is that this is a good way to get to know better the person that he or she is considering marrying. Maybe the two could attend instruction in the Catholic Faith together. It could be a great opportunity to discuss each other's religious beliefs and expectations. If, after studying and praying, one decides to make another leap, a leap of faith into the Catholic Church, then it is because one has really understood the issues and freely decided to take on the divine commitments of love. One should not convert just to please another person. Certainly we should avoid putting undue pressure on anyone to convert.

Again, the more you know about the person you plan to marry, the freer you are in making this decision. I don't know any married couple that ever said that they had learned too much about each other before they were married. On the contrary, many have said they wished they had known this or that about the other person while they were dating, because if they had, they would never have married that person.

Margie: That's sad.

Father JP: Well, that is why it is so important to be straight-forward with each other. Too many couples rush into marriage thinking, "We love each other very much. We will deal with each other's defects and those deeper concerns later — our love will get us through them all."

It is much better to thoroughly get to know each other, not hiding matters that later will become a source of contention. You don't want the other to think that he or she was fooled into marrying you. On the contrary, you want your future spouse to be able to say that he or she chose to marry you just the way you are.

Sam: But Margie told me that you said that she would be marrying Christ in the person she marries. But if she married a Jew like myself, how could she love Christ through me? How could I represent Christ for her? Isn't this an obstacle to us in considering marriage?

Father JP: Christ was a faithful Jew like you. He also said that anything you do for someone in need, you do to Him (Matthew 25:40). Thus you could still represent Christ for Margie.

Moreover, Margie would represent Christ in loving you. As Christ had a great love for the Jews, He would be expressing that ongoing love for his people every time Margie would show her love to you — if the two of you married, of course.

Now you can see why the prohibition of marrying someone outside the Catholic Faith is not absolute.

Margie: That's makes a lot of sense, Father JP. Are there other issues that are important for us to discuss beforehand?

Father JP: Certainly a couple should discuss their vision for the family and how they plan to raise the children. What is appropriate and inappropriate discipline? What help and role does each one expect of the other? Do you expect to send your children to public, private, or parochial schools? It is very important to share the same values and vision of the family.

They should also discuss how they want to approach having children. Do they want to wait before having the first child? How long should they wait before having the next? How they plan to go about that waiting — through complete abstinence, Natural Family Planning, or contraception? Again, they should consider each other's religious values in making that decision. Even though one may accept the use of one or another of the means, it is possible that an excessive desire for sex, or a reawakening of one's religious beliefs, may change that attitude later. It is extremely important to be totally up front and honest with one another on these points.

Must We Have Children as Soon as We Get Married?

Sam: Your comments seem to imply that couples start having children right after they marry. To me, that seems a little rash. It might be better to wait until they adjust to one another, they get settled in their new home, and they put finances in order.

Father JP: Although there are some advantages in waiting, there are many good reasons for a couple to be open to begin having children from the start. Of course, the Church does not mandate anything on this matter.

First, it is a sign that the couple knows and accepts the mission they have received from God, a mission to go out and bear fruit together. They have not come to selfishly seek pleasure from each other or just to give each other companionship, but to give themselves unconditionally to each other with an openness to new life. It is a mission to raise that new life in the Faith, to direct and prepare that new life for its mission in life.

Second, it is a real ratification of the love that the two of them have for each other. When a new child comes into this world, it is a real personification of the love that the spouses have for each other: the two become one and that new "oneness" takes on its own name nine months later.

150

Third, often difficulties arise between the two spouses in the first year or two of marriage. This is the moment when they make the biggest adjustment in their lives: to live in a committed relationship to another imperfect human being. At times one of the spouses may find it all too easy to walk out of the commitment. Having a child dependent on the two of you for its future happiness may encourage each to forget his or her pride and to find a way to make up.

Sam: But this doesn't mean we can't decide to wait, does it?

Father JP: No. You would have to rely on some licit means to do so, however, like Natural Family Planning or complete abstinence. This is not something that the Church would recommend as a way to start a marriage. You wouldn't want to separate the intense spiritual experience of the wedding from the intense emotional experience of the physical self-giving, unless you really had no other choice.

What about the Number of Children?

Margie: Father JP, what about the size of the family: are we really free to say how many children we can have? I thought the Church said that we must have as many children as possible.

Father JP: The Church has never said that a couple should have the maximum number of children possible. Women should not be treated as baby factories; God does not require them to churn out a child every nine or ten months.

There are various ways that God uses to naturally space out children and limit the number of children that a couple receives. One way is that God limits the fertility of some couples, so that they may only be able to have one or two children or even none at all. He does not do this because He loves them less, but because He has other plans for them.

Another way God uses to naturally space children is breast-feeding.

Sam: Come on, JP, you don't really think breast-feeding actually helps space children, do you? Or are you saying that it somehow works to suppress the woman's desire for sex? But isn't that somewhat unfair to the man?

Father JP: No, Sam, that's not how it works. When a woman breast-feeds her child, that tells her body that a child depends on it for nutrition. The body usually responds by keeping the woman infertile. This is no old wives' tale, but is backed by scientific research.[16] Granted, this may not be effective for a handful of women, but there is more and more research being done to show how breast-feeding can be used effectively, what works and what doesn't, and how nutrition also affects breast-feeding and fertility.[17] This kind of research has been neglected until recently since little money is to be made from promoting breast-feeding whereas contraceptives and baby formula can be big business.

Margie: Could a couple limit the number of children to two or three? They might not think they could handle more.

Father JP: I don't think it is wise to be calculating with our love. We should want to manifest our love with generosity, in as many ways as possible. To say that you only want two incarnations of your love for each other is like saying that you only want one or two pictures of your wedding since it would cost so much money to have more.

I also think it is wrong to make blanket statements, like saying that we cannot afford any more children, or we only want two or three, or we can only handle so many. If the couple has significant reasons, they may say, "*At this point in time* it would be imprudent to have another child, but if circumstances change, we would be open to more." Thus, they are not imposing their will upon God.

A couple should always try to make this decision with generosity and according to God's will. They should look at each child as a gift from Him and not a burden.

No thanks, let's not overdo it. We have enough already!

Margie: But having received a gift of two or three children, couldn't a couple say that's enough for us?

Father JP: If someone gave you a hundred dollars one week and then came up to you a few weeks later and offered to give you another gift of a hundred dollars, would you say, "No, no, no! I can't handle any more money. That first hundred dollars was more than enough"?

Margie: No, of course not.

Father JP: Well, if we really look upon children as gifts, we would welcome each one no matter how many we already have, just as we wouldn't refuse to accept a new gift from someone just because we've received one or two gifts from him already. Each gift should be received joyfully and with thanksgiving.

A Christian believer — a good Jewish believer too — would trust God's providence, that God would provide for the family who turns to Him with faith. If we really believe that God loves us as His dear children, then we should have no fear. Only those without faith will be calculating and stingy.

However, one shouldn't put undue burdens on one's spouse or on the family as a whole. Thus, for serious reasons the Church acknowledges it as part of God's plan that couples recognize periods of their infertility and use that knowledge to avoid putting undue burden on the other spouse or on the family. This acknowledges that periodic infertility is part of a woman's feminine character — that she is not pure fertility — and respects the meaning of the marital union.

Sam: So, JP, you say that we should discuss all these matters before marriage as a way to really get to know one another. I agree that focusing on these matters may help us to focus on other things besides just getting physical. Nevertheless, becoming more intimate spiritually could lead us to become more intimate physically. We have already had troubles with that. I foresee it becoming harder rather than easier.

Father JP: You have a point, Sam. It is not enough just to have good desires and to date with the focus on getting to know each other. However, the more you get to know Margie as a person, the more respect you will have for her. As you get to know her better, the more motivated you will be to respect her in body and spirit.

However, it is still important to use the means that we discussed earlier: avoiding situations where physical intimacy can take place and helping each other with moderation in the signs of affection for each other.

Margie: We'll keep working on this, Father JP.

Sam: Yes, we'll keep trying. Thank you again.

Personal Struggles

Several weeks pass before Margie returns to Father JP's confessional. She has more questions about how she can better live out her courtship with Sam. Also, concerns over Sam's religion have come to the forefront.

Dating a Non-Catholic

Margie: Father JP, this is Margie again. Thank you for hearing my confession. Do you mind if I ask you something?

Father JP: No, Margie, go right ahead.

Margie: Sam and I have talked a lot more about what we have in common and how we differ. Actually, we agree on most things. However, after our last conversation, I can't picture myself marrying a person who is not Catholic, especially after what you said about marrying a person whom I would choose to be my father. I love Sam a lot, but I'm afraid to tell him this.

Father JP: This is a good desire you have. Tertullian, an early Christian writer, wrote:

> *How can I ever express the happiness of the marriage that is joined together by the church, strengthened by an offering, sealed by a blessing, announced by angels and ratified by the Father? ... How wonderful the bond between two believers, with a single hope, a single desire, a single observance, a single service! They are both brethren and both fellow servants; there is no separation between*

155

them in spirit or flesh. In fact, they are truly two in one flesh, and where the flesh is one, one is the spirit.[18]

Sam is a very fine man. He is quite virtuous and noble. But you cannot be afraid to lose him. He is not yours. Even though it is difficult, be frank with him and tell him of your decision. If he is willing to explore the Catholic Faith, perhaps he can take the doctrinal classes we talked about. Even so, you must be ready to let go of him, follow your conscience and let him follow his. You must respect his decision if he chooses not to become a Catholic. Let us pray for him, for his decision, and for strength for you to do what is right.

Margie: I know you are right, but it won't be easy.

Father JP: Doing what is right is never easy. Pray, asking for the strength to follow through. Also pray for Sam — that he may respect your conscience and follow his own, and that he may come to the fullness of the truth.

Modesty: Guarding My Treasured Gift

Margie: Father JP, I will.

Also, Father, what should I do when he makes hints about wearing more provocative dress or swimwear? On the one hand, I feel great that he is attracted to me; on the other hand, I feel a little guilty. Am I being prudish?

Father JP: No. It is your natural instinct to be modest. Modesty is Nature's way to safeguard this treasure of our self-gift for the one person to whom we choose to give ourselves for the rest of our lives. We all have a natural desire to be loved — to be loved as a person — and not to be used as an object.

Suppose your brother received a very expensive bike as a gift. What would happen if he just left it out on the front lawn after he finished riding it?

Margie: It would be stolen, of course.

Father JP: What would he do to prevent it from being stolen?

156

A treasured gift?

Margie: He should lock it up or put it in the garage, keeping it safe and out of sight.

Father JP: What if someone who loved you gave you a very expensive diamond necklace, would you put it on a table on the sidewalk outside your home so that the people passing by could look at it and admire it?

Margie: No, of course not. Someone would steal that too.

Father JP: Then what would you do with it?

157

Margie: If I were not wearing it, I'd put it in a hidden and safe place. If I had a safe, I'd lock it up there.

Father JP: Well, the gift of your very self, which your body represents, is much more valuable than a diamond necklace or an expensive bike. It is priceless. Yet we can show it off as if we didn't care who took it or what they would do with it. If we want people to respect the gift of our self, then we must guard it well.

It is amazing how much respect goes along with being well dressed. When a young man or woman dresses well, others just naturally treat them with more respect, calling them by expressions like, "Excuse me, sir" or "Excuse me, miss" instead of "Hey, kid." Modest dress also makes it easier for men to see a real person in a woman's body rather than a sex object. When you dress modestly Sam and others will treat you and your body with respect.

Much the same can be said about being modest in speech. It helps foster a real respect for the sacredness of the human body and sexuality.

Margie: I get the idea, Father JP, but it's hard being the only person who tries to live the virtue of modesty. People start calling you "Sister So'n'So," or saying, "Here comes the saint." I want to be attractive to men.

Father JP: And indeed, you ought. But what kind of man do you want to attract? Someone who will use and abuse you as if you were a...?

Margie: No!

Father JP: What kind of man do you want to attract — someone who will be a good spouse for you and a good father of your children, remember?

Margie: Yes, that's right.

Father JP: It is good to remember that the sense of being loved or desired physically or even the feeling of being connected to another person emotionally can cloud over our desire to be

158

loved as a person and can break down our natural sense of shame and modesty. All this endangers the precious gift that we are.

Look at the Eucharist. See how we treat it. We reserve the Body of Christ in the tabernacle, a strong metal box that we lock with a key so no one will be able to break in and steal Our Lord. We put the consecrated hosts in a golden ciborium that we usually cover with a veil because it is sacred. Even the tabernacle itself is covered with a veil to show us that there is something sacred inside. Well, our body is something very sacred. It is the material dimension of our gift of self. We need to preserve this sacredness and keep it from being violated by the eyes and imagination of others.

Modesty tells others that we desire to be loved as a person: "You must not touch me, not even in your inner most secret thoughts and desires until I become part of you and you of me."

Besides, Margie, what does a young woman think about when she notices that some guys are gawking at her?

Margie: She is thinking, "Gee, these guys like me. I'm an attractive woman." It makes her feel good that she has something to offer men.

Father JP: Yes, Margie, you're right. But do you notice how this causes her to become preoccupied with herself? A woman usually starts analyzing in detail what it is in her appearance and dress that attracts the guys to her. She may do the same with the different parts of her anatomy. She starts moving the body in such a way to tantalize the guys even further and draw more attention to herself. The fact is, it causes her to become focused on herself and less on others.

A great side effect of modesty is that it actually helps us not to focus on ourselves, making it easier for us to think about others. Modesty draws out our selfishness and self-centeredness.

This is true with men too, by the way. We can also be quite vain and self-centered. We need to live the virtue of modesty just as much as women do, especially in our speech. Men tend to draw attention to themselves by showing off their muscles and chest hairs, or by saying provocative things to point out their masculinity.

Margie: OK, Father JP, I get it.

TV and Movies

Father JP: By the way, Margie, do you watch TV or go to the movies?

Margie: Well, I watch a movie once or twice a month, and I try to follow one of the soaps. Why do you ask?

Father JP: What do you do when something offensive comes on the screen?

Margie: Nothing, usually. Occasionally I may turn my head or something. Is there something wrong with that?

Father JP: What do you think Our Lord would do? Suppose Jesus sat down next to you as you turned on the television or as you went to watch a movie at a theater. While you were watching the movie together, a scene comes on that is offensive to His Blessed Mother. What do you think Our Lord would do?

Margie: Walk out?

Father JP: That is the least I think he would do. Do you remember what Jesus did when He entered the Temple and saw people buying and selling things there? What did He do?

Margie: He got upset.

Father JP: Not only did he get upset, he reacted very strongly, even violently: he started turning over their tables, dumping their money on the ground, breaking the cages that the animals were in and chasing the vendors out of the Temple. Why? Because they were doing something that was offensive to His Heavenly Father, turning His Father's house of prayer into a marketplace (John 2:13–17).

160

Oh, Jesus!

Well, I think that Our Lord would do something similar if he saw a scene on television or in a movie that he found offensive to His Blessed Mother. I think He would become very angry. I can even picture Him becoming violent like He did in the Temple. I could see Him getting so mad that he would pick up the TV and toss it out the window. He would at least get up and walk out or turn off the TV.

Margie: Wait a minute, Father JP, don't you think that's a bit fanatical?

Father JP (*There was a moment of silence as Margie waited for Father JP to respond*): Perhaps you are right. It is hard to predict how Our Lord would react in this particular situation. The point is, however, that he would not just passively put up with material that is offensive to His Mother and degrading for all of us. Besides walking out or turning off the television, He might speak up and tell us how our love for God would not allow us to accept such offensive material. He may even indicate that we should get rid of the TV altogether.

So when you go to a movie or watch TV with Jesus and one of those indecent scenes comes on the screen, if we see Jesus get up and walk out and we don't, or we don't turn off the TV, then we are not followers of Jesus Christ.

Margie: What about when we go to the theater to watch a movie? If we walk out, then it means wasting the money we paid for it.

Father JP: Just do what Jesus would do. You could request a refund, but I doubt that the theater will be receptive to that request. One thing I would suggest is that you try to read the reviews and check out the movies ahead of time, before you lay out money to watch a bad show.

Margie: I guess you're right, but all I can promise is that I'll try.

Father JP: That's all that I can ask and that's all that the Lord asks.

Unhealthy Relationships

Sam accompanied Margie while she waited in line to go to confession. While Margie talks to Father JP, Sam remains outside. A person comes up behind Sam just as Margie leaves the confessional and gives Sam a nudge to encourage him to go in. Although he had not planned on entering the confessional, he does so because the unknown penitent behind him urged him forward.

Sam: Hello, JP, since I am here with Margie I thought I'd stop in to ask you about something you said last time that just doesn't sit well with me.

162

Father JP: What's that, Sam?

Sam: You said that a man should look for a mother in choosing a wife. That doesn't seem right.

Father JP: What bothers you about it?

Sam: It just seems strange that I, or anyone else, should be looking to replace his mother with someone else. It reminded me of when I dated a girl in college who seemed to be looking for someone to be her father. She wasn't interested in romance except when it brought her someone who could tell her what to do, make decisions for her, bail her out when she was in trouble, reassure her self-esteem — the list goes on. It seems that she never had much of a relationship with her own father and so she was using boyfriends to fill that gap.

I hate to say this, but I dropped her as soon as I realized that. I just didn't want to get mixed up with someone so needy. She seemed a little wacky to me.

Father JP: Perhaps I need to clarify myself. A woman should not be looking for a man to replace a father or to fill some emotional need for fatherly affection, especially if she somehow missed out on this while growing up. Nor should a man look for a woman to fill emotional needs not met as a child. A person in this situation is not ready to marry; in fact, the individual is probably not even in right conditions to date. Such a person ought to resolve his or her issues before beginning any serious dating.

What I intended to say was that a man ought to look to his mother (or someone else who is a good mother) to discern those qualities that would qualify a woman as a good mother, because he is choosing her to be the mother of his children. Likewise, a woman should look to her father (or someone else who is a good father) to discern those qualities that would qualify a man to be a good father for her children. I mentioned this to help you and Margie think about and discuss those qualities in a mate that are important to make marriage work.

Sam: OK, I see what you mean. But then what do you do if a woman is really looking for someone to replace her father? Or, what if she is looking to replace her mother instead of her father? I mean, does that ever happen?

Father JP: These situations can and do happen. If a woman grows up with a very poor relationship with her mother or father, this can produce a psychological void and with it a tendency to fill or replace that failed relationship with a substitute. Many unhealthy relationships and marriages begin in this way, motivated by a desire to replace a poor child-parent relationship. Many homosexual relationships seem to develop in this way too.[19]

Sam: But is this a reason to avoid relationships or to put off getting married?

Father JP: Earlier we spoke about why God made sexual experience so intense. Do you remember?

Sam: How could I forget? I keep it in mind every time I start thinking about sex; I want to make my wedding night special.

Father JP: The intensity of the sexual emotions are very effective to help a man and woman bond, etching their spiritual bond and their commitment of love into each one's psyche.

Well, the same thing can happen in childhood. If a child is sexually abused, that experience gets etched into his psyche, along with the emotions of fear, anger, anxiety, guilt — even self-hatred. The same could happen when a child experiences some other intense or traumatic experience, for example, if a child feels emotionally abandoned, betrayed, or ignored by one or both parents.

For example, one woman I knew grew up with a father who was verbally abusive, and sometimes physically abusive, to her and to her mother. Her mother was weak and passive; she didn't defend herself or this little girl. This girl grew to resent her mother and her passivity, and she became attracted to her father's strength and power. She was instinctively drawn to athletics, developing physical strength and emotional toughness, yet deep down inside she remained a little child who longed for a tender and intimate relationship with the mother, an intimacy she never experienced.

The more these deep-seated emotional longings are hidden from others, the more they may affect the way a person relates to others. This girl's deep and hidden desire for that missing relationship with her mother caused her to unconsciously seek a romantic and sexual relationship with another woman to replace the broken one. But instead of filling the void, it just masked one set of emotions with another; it may mask the desire for a good, loving daughter-mother relationship with an intense sexual one. However, this can only last so long before the suppressed emotions rise to the surface again in the form of depression, guilt, and self-hatred.

If these deep emotions and hidden desires end up controlling one's decisions and motivating one's relationships, then the individual is clearly not ready for marriage and filling the responsibilities of a spouse and parent. Moreover, it would be dangerous for such a person to enter into a dating relationship or vocational discernment when these emotions dominate their motivation and blind their good reason.

Sam: JP, now that you mention homosexuality, I have a Catholic friend from high school that is really angry with the Church over this issue. Why does the Catholic Church have a hang-up with homosexuality?

Father JP: Sam, there is a lot to this question — much more than we can cover in the confessional, especially if there are others in line. Perhaps you and your friend can make an appointment and we can get together to discuss this matter in depth. There is quite a bit to this issue.

Sam: That's fair. I'll see if my friend is interested.

Learning to Communicate

A number of weeks go by before Margie and Sam return. Margie attempted to break things off, but Sam promised to keep the relationship pure. He even suggested an openness to explore the Catholic Faith. His response gave Margie new hope and enthusiasm for the relationship, causing her to rethink her decision.

Margie and Sam made quite an effort to remain chaste and tried to create a fun and more enriching dating experience, discussing many of the issues that Father JP brought up in the previous session. However, they still had a little setback in their efforts to avoid passionate kissing and touching.

Male and Female Differences

Sam: JP, I give up. We've tried. This pure love business is a nice theory, but I think it is just impossible to put into practice.

Father JP: What's the matter?

Sam: We've tried, but it's just too hard. The reality is, whenever we get together I feel drawn to get physical with Margie. We resisted for a while — it just seems like I can't help myself. Then afterward I feel guilty, as though I have betrayed Margie and the commitment we made to wait until marriage. Maybe Margie would be better off with someone else more worthy of her love.

Margie: It's not your fault, Sam. I have never met anyone as worthy as you — I'm the one who needs to be stronger than I've been. We can't give up now.

Sam: Thanks for that vote of confidence, Margie, but it just seems impossible. We've been trying to have a positive focus on each date, avoiding being alone, but we can't hide our passionate episode a few days back from JP. I was the one that came on strong to you. I just couldn't say no.

You know, JP, sometimes you're tired from a long week of work and behind on sleep. You just don't feel like struggling and you give in without thinking.

Margie: You're right, Sam, but I could have been stronger. It's hard for me too.

Father JP, can you help us? We have been very good the last few weeks except for this incident where we just got carried away. Even this time we started in a very innocent and decent way, but before we knew it, we were passionately kissing and getting physically intimate. Is there anything else we can do? I really want to be able to show him how much I love him while keeping things pure.

Father JP: Perhaps all you both need is just a good night's sleep. Sometimes, Sam, it just might be better to call Margie and tell her you are exhausted and that it would better to wait until tomorrow.

Sam: But I don't want to disappoint Margie — or myself. We both look forward to getting together. If I don't show up, she will be disappointed. If I show up and then we go too far, she will be disappointed.

Margie: Sam, I know I overreact sometimes, especially when I've been waiting all week to see you. But if you were to call me and say that you needed a good night's sleep, I think I would accept that — at least I'd try.

Father JP: First, I am proud of the two of you for making this difficult commitment. Let's not be surprised that these efforts of yours are hard to live out at times. We don't get any support from the media or our society. Even our families can make it difficult for us. But there are many worthwhile things in life that are difficult, like getting a college education or training to be a professional athlete. It would be much easier to skip college and to go into some manual trade or just watch sports on television, but if we have talent, we should make the effort to do something more productive with our lives.

So we need to help one another live out this ideal of a wholesome and pure love. In doing so, however, it helps to remember our differences, that women and men tend to react to sexual advances in different ways and for different reasons. Men should get to know the weaknesses and fears of women and women should get to know the weaknesses and fears of men. Then, with these in mind, we will be better able to help each other overcome and avoid them.

Sam: That sounds a bit old fashioned, almost sexist. Everyone now recognizes that men and women are equal and basically the same.

Margie: I tend to agree with Sam, Father JP. Our society seems to be ahead of the Catholic Church in this.

Father JP: Men and women are equal in dignity, but different in their physical and psychological makeup. Their equality is based on being equally children of God and destined for union with God in heaven. That does not mean that men and women are identical.

Men can never become mothers and bear children in their womb. That's just a fact. It's not a matter of being sexist. We are just pointing to the facts of this difference. The difference between man and woman is not just physical; it is also manifested in our behavior and how we react to sensuality. Men and women also communicate, and establish and maintain relationships differently. For example, I'm sure you have noticed that boys relate to their fathers differently than to their mothers. Girls also relate differently to their brothers than to their sisters. Girls relate to

168

I'm due in two weeks. What about you?

girls and guys to guys differently than girls and guys do to each other. It's not that one way or relating is better than another, they are just different.

In recent years, a number of secular and Christian authors have become quite popular in pointing out these differences. John Gray, for example, is a secular psychologist who wrote the book *Men Are from Mars, Women Are from Venus.*[20] By pointing out how men and women think and communicate differently, he is able to successfully help couples improve their relationship. Deborah Tannen, a professor of linguistics at Georgetown University, published her research on how men and women think and speak differently in her popular book, *You Just Don't Understand: Women and Men in Conversation.*[21] Gary

Smalley, a Christian marriage counselor, has written several books helping men and women understand their differences in order to produce lasting marriages or to recover broken ones.[22] Other authors have also found that recognizing and respecting the differences between men and women is key to healthy relationships.

Sam: And what are those differences? Do you mean to say that men are stronger and women weaker, or that men are calm and logical, whereas women are more intuitive and emotional? I just don't buy that.

Father JP: Often, especially in times of crisis, it is the woman who is stronger. Moreover, men can be just as emotional as women. For instance, when men look at an attractive woman, their emotions are aroused and they end up doing and saying some very illogical things. Men can also be quite intuitive when it comes to problem solving.

But putting the stereotypes aside, Sam, men and women are different in many ways. For example, psychologists note that women are biologically and emotionally oriented toward being mothers and naturally place more importance on establishing the type of relationship that will ensure a secure and stable environment for raising children. Women are naturally sensitive to those actions that have repercussions on the establishment and maintenance of family relations.

Men are less relationship oriented and more "object" or "thing" oriented. A man is naturally inclined to be a protector and provider, therefore he has to be able to interact with the world of objects to avoid potential dangers and to get what is needed to sustain a family.

Did you ever notice how women tend to identify themselves by relationships? "I'm Jack's wife" or "I'm Joey's mother." Men, on the other hand, identify themselves by what they do or accomplish. A man would identify himself by saying, "I'm an engineer who designs airplanes" or "I won the Nobel Peace Prize in 1989."

Male-female differences: a win-win situation

Regardless whether or not you think this is something that should change, it's a fact of life that most men and most women identify themselves in this way.

Men enjoy competition and tend to judge each other on how well each one performs a given task: comparing physical strength, intellectual mastery, and professional success, for example. Women love to create and share experiences with others, although they do tend to compete for attention and over how attractive they are, which are relationship-developing attributes.

Sam: But some women are just as competitive as men in the intellectual and professional world, even in the world of sports.

Father JP: Yes, and some men are good at relationships. These qualities are acquired and learned; it is just that men are more naturally inclined one way and women another. And this shows up in how we communicate as well.

Sam: How so? Men and women mean the same thing when they speak.

Father JP: Not necessarily. Take the phrase, "Let's just be friends." A guy often says this to a girl when he senses that the girl is not ready for a deeper commitment. He is basically saying that he likes a girl and that he hopes something will work out between the two of them. He is leaving the door open for something to develop in the future.

When a girl says, "Let's just be friends," she is saying that it's over and there's absolutely no hope for the relationship in the future. She is trying to be nice, she doesn't want to hurt the guy, but she has made up her mind; the door is closed.

Sam: I think you're on to something here.

A Weakness for Passion or Romance

Margie: But Father JP, what does this have to do with keeping our dating pure? Let's face it, both women and men have a strong passion for sex. In this we are equal, wouldn't you say?

Father JP: Yes, men and women have strong sexual passions, but in different ways; men and women react differently to sexual advances and stimuli. For instance, men tend to have a very strong sex drive that is easily triggered, especially by visual stimuli. And because the connection between sexual pleasure and its relational meaning is weak in men, they tend to treat women as objects rather than as persons. Just look at the way many men tend to "size up" a woman according to her sex appeal without considering her intellectual ability or personality traits. Men judge a woman much like how they would a juicy beefsteak. This also explains why pornography is so prevalent among men.

Margie: Sam is not like that with me.

Sam: I hope not, Margie, but JP is right. Many men are that way. Some of the guys that I know are real animals in the way they treat women.

Father JP: It shouldn't surprise us that men tend to objectivize women since they naturally objectivize everything else, even their own sexual appetites.

It is true that we are describing general tendencies. A particular man may have overcome certain male weaknesses and acquired qualities that women have more naturally. Likewise, a particular woman may have acquired some masculine strengths or weaknesses. So don't think that a man or a woman is stuck to a general gender profile. But it can give us insights into ourselves and others, as well as help us learn how to better communicate and help one another be better.

Women have many natural qualities that are oriented toward a healthy relationship. For example, they have a greater desire for a secure and lasting relationship. This is natural, since if a woman gets pregnant, she will likely become very dependent on a man to provide for her and her child. So the idea of having sexual intercourse outside the context of a meaningful relationship and commitment is practically unthinkable for a woman. That is why male prostitutes for women are virtually unheard of and women addicted to pornography are quite rare.

If a man gets a woman pregnant he can run away, whereas a woman can't. This means that women have a greater interest in being responsible. Part of this responsibility is that of "taming" men and their weakness for passion. We can say that men learn fatherhood from women.[23] Women teach men to be good fathers by helping them to see that there are real people behind their sensual attraction.

Women can help men overcome their selfishness and to be generous in their self-giving by not letting themselves be used as objects of men's desires. To be a good father means being willing to take on responsibility, so a woman ought to be able to say, "If you want to have sex with me, then you must show that you are ready to take on the responsibility of providing and caring for what sex may bring, that is, that you are committed to me and my future children for life." A woman "tames" and teaches a man fatherhood by saving physical intimacy until marriage.

Sam: It seems you're blaming male selfishness for all the difficulties in keeping a relationship pure. That seems a bit one-sided. Women can be selfish too.

Father JP: I am not blaming men; I am just pointing out what our weaknesses are. We can and ought to help others where they are weakest, and we can most benefit from their help in those areas where we are weak. Women have weaknesses just as we do, and we can help compensate for their weaknesses as they ought to compensate for ours. Men tend to be weak where women are strong and vice versa.

Because women are relationship oriented, their weakness is for romance. They are less sensitive to visual stimuli and more sensitive to what they hear. It means a lot to a woman to hear, "I love you." A woman may fall prey to a man's word by letting her imagination go into a tizzy over the possibility that a man really likes her and is attracted to her. A man can easily manipulate a woman in this way to get what he wants.

Women also tend to share with each other their romantic moments. A woman listening to another describing her experiences imagines how she would feel if she were in a similar situation with her own boyfriend. The fantasy can be so vivid that it is almost the same as if it really happened. This is why romance novels, soap operas, and romantic movies are as dangerous for a woman as pornography is for a man.

This fantasizing makes the woman prone to put herself into a compromising romantic situation, even though she intends to keep things in check. For example, say a woman watches a movie about a girl and a painter who fall in love with each other. He convinces her to let him paint her nude. The movie portrays the painter with a kind of innocent delight for the girl's beauty. Watching the movie, the woman imagines herself in the girl's place, fantasizing about what a wonderful thing it would be to be admired in the same way as the girl was in the movie. Then she wonders whether her boyfriend would have the same kind of innocent delight in seeing her in the nude. You can imagine what this woman is setting herself up for.

174

Another example of the danger of romantic fantasy is one in which a man presents the possibility of a romantic excursion to his girlfriend. It may seem innocent, but it really isn't prudent. Perhaps the man suggests to his girlfriend that the two of them go on a camping trip together — in the fresh air, in beautiful mountains. He'd protect her from the bears and other predators. Of course, "We'll use separate sleeping bags, and there'll be one or two other couples." And she thinks, "How romantic!" Men will put up with a little romance when they anticipate some sensual satisfaction. But that's precisely when things get out of hand and they end up going beyond their bounds.

Margie: Father, that's kind of what happened with us, although it was not that disastrous. I thought that it would be nice to have Sam over for a nice, romantic candlelight dinner. This was something that a friend of mine had done with her boyfriend. Of course, after our dinner, since we were all alone, things just got out of hand with passionate kissing and hugging.

Father JP: Sam, that is why you have to help Margie by suggesting safer romantic situations, ones in which you know nothing will happen. You should find ways to please her, even making them romantic, but always keeping the situation safe and appropriate. Also, ask her to be a good mother to you, aware of your needs and weaknesses.

Sam: Are you saying that Margie and I shouldn't vacation together? Isn't that a great opportunity to get to know one another and discuss important issues?

Father JP: It wouldn't be a wise idea. Besides, what makes the honeymoon so special is that it would be your first vacation together.

All sorts of situations can arise when an unmarried couple takes an unchaperoned vacation together. If something goes wrong or something unexpected occurs, you don't have your normal support structure of friends and family to help you out or protect you from some inappropriate situation, like the camping trip. You may intend on doing things correctly, like getting separate hotel rooms, for instance, but then you discover the price of the hotel rooms is more than expected, or that they only have one vacancy. The safest way to go is to wait or to make sure that it is well chaperoned.

Margie: Is there anything I can do to help Sam and I avoid risky situations?

Father JP: For starters, Margie, you would do well to avoid fantasy. If you do daydream, keep it short and don't allow it to touch on actions that would be inappropriate on a movie screen. Better yet, avoid any fantasy that you would be ashamed of if someone else were reading your mind, since God is indeed privy to our thoughts.

Now, when you show your affection to Sam, do it in ways that respect his male sensitivity. A warm, secure embrace may not be a problem for you, but may easily trigger Sam's sensuality. You would also do well to suggest doing activities that Sam likes and finds exciting. Some men like attending sporting events; others like air, boat, or auto shows; still others like to be in the great outdoors. Try to find ways that will bring Sam some excitement without exciting his sensuality. Besides, those experiences will come in very handy when you are married and you want to renew the romance of your courting days. Didn't we talk about this last time?

Margie: Yes, we did. You mentioned how the romantic dating experiences can be recreated to bring back some excitement and romance to the marriage. You even inferred that married couples could get bored or even tired of sex. But I found that pretty difficult to believe. How can sex become boring?

Father JP: You may find it hard now, but you might if you were married, had one or two kids, and found yourself exhausted every day due to the uninterrupted care of the children and the house, or if you had to deal with a husband who came home tired after a long day's work and who didn't want to do anything to help out with chores or kids. How would you react then, if he insisted on having a good, hot meal each and every night and then marital relations with you after you put the kids to bed?

Sam: Do men really treat their wives like that? That seems to be just an old-fashioned caricature.

Why Is the Sex Drive So Strong and So Different?

Father JP: Some men certainly can and do. I've heard quite a number of married women complain of this. Since the sex drive in men is more intense and constant than for women, they naturally desire to satisfy it more frequently. A woman's drive goes up and down with her fertility, energy level, and emotions. Women often resent having a husband who doesn't take an interest in their children, who comes home from work and plops himself down in a chair without lifting a finger to help out with the household chores. If she doesn't get the feeling that he understands her tiredness and her efforts to please him and care for the kids, then she finds it hard to reciprocate when he takes a sexual interest in her. She resents that expectation to be there sexually for him night after night. She feels like she is being used.

Margie: Some women complain about that. They resent how their husbands just seem to be interested in sexual gratification. They complain how they miss the magic of dating when he'd bring her flowers, or he'd take her out and do certain things to make her feel special. Can a woman do anything to prevent her marriage from degenerating to the point where she feels she is being "used" by her husband?

Father JP: It's a matter of mutual respect. A man must learn to respect his wife by showing with actions how he appreciates her responsiveness when she gives herself intimately to him, that he realizes that her gift of self to him is entirely free.

Sam: I think a man should also make sure that he is not forcing himself on his wife, maybe by asking her whether she is in the mood and not presuming that she is.

Father JP: Yes, Sam, that is important. Proper respect recognizes that freedom and doesn't take it for granted.

A man also shows this respect when he links his own self-gift to a gift expressed in service and responsiveness to her needs. When a married woman sees her husband sensitive to her needs, she is naturally more sensitive to his.

Likewise, a woman must respect her husband and his natural tendencies, and direct them to his good and the good of the family.

Margie: How does a married woman do that?

Father JP: First, it is good for a married woman to recognize and respect that God gave men a strong and constant sex-drive, and that God designed men this way for a purpose.

Margie: I can see how God designed it so that a man and woman's first intense sexual experience would take place on their wedding night, as you said, so that their strong emotions would engrave their commitment permanently into their psyche. But why would God give men such an insatiable sex drive if it only seems to lead men to abuse their wives?

Father JP: It seems that God has designed things the way He has to help men focus on their families and to get them away from the worries of their work.

Let's face it, men have a tendency to get wrapped up in their work. They can get stressed out and worry about making enough money to meet the family's needs. Some men fear that they are insufficiently productive at work and may be fired or laid off. Other men are very ambitious for success. This causes both types of men to dwell extensively on how to improve the results of their work, and to achieve this they tend to work ever longer and longer hours, often to the detriment of their health, marriage, and family.

It seems that God gave man an intense and constant sex drive to help him escape this trap. Through this natural drive, God draws a man away from his work so that he may focus on the reasons for doing his work — his wife and family. It is God's natural way to motivate him to engage his wife and to do so in such a way that she will be willing to be there for him.

The intensity of the emotional experience can even have a druglike effect that may help both him and his wife to forget their worries and to get the rest they need to start the next day refreshed.

Margie: You said that a woman can use this to direct her husband toward the good of the family. How so? You seem to be describing a compulsive, almost animalistic behavior.

Father JP: It doesn't have to be so base. If a woman tells her husband that she'd be in a much more romantic mood for him if he'd be more communicative when he came home, or if he'd help her out with the dishes or in putting the kids to bed, then her husband might just take her at her word and see how she'd respond when he does those things for her. If she indeed was more romantic and in the mood for him, then he'd likely become more communicative or helpful around the house.

Moreover, keeping her husband's "weakness" in mind, a good woman will make an effort to remain attractive because she does not want that intense and constant sex drive to get misdirected toward some other woman.

Sam: Why would God do this with the sex drive and not with the other passions?

Father JP: In a sense, God does.

Take the passion for food, for example. If a man only had a slab of raw meat and a raw potato to eat, he would probably find them sufficiently edible and nutritious to sustain his health, but that would be very unattractive to eat. However, a savory, well-cooked, and presentable meal brings a man to join himself to other people, attracting him not only to eat for his physical health, but also to share his time and attention with others — with his wife and children who share the meal, and with extended family members for a bigger and fancier holiday meal.

Sam: Is this just a one-way street? What about things that a man should do to respect his wife and meet her desires?

Father JP: Women hate being taken for granted. We men assume, "She knows I love her. I work so hard, and I have done so much for her." We just don't get it. Women focus much more on the little things, the compliments, the little details of service.

Margie: Men don't get this, do they, Father JP? They seem to think that sex is all there is.

Father JP: We men tend to focus on the big things, on the grand accomplishments. We think we have shown our love when we do something big for our love. We don't realize that little things are extremely important to women. Remembering anniversaries, like when you first met, or your first kiss, means a lot. A man who opens a door, who is courteous and has good manners, one who corrects another man for using foul or inappropriate language in front of his girlfriend or wife, is very appreciated. Women get upset when those little things are neglected and their efforts are taken for granted.

Husbands can avoid provoking this kind of reaction by trying to make their wives feel special, surprising them with a gift from time to time. That gift can be as simple as flowers or a box of chocolates, jewelry or a special honeymoon-type trip, which would surprise her even more.

When it comes to marital intimacy, I remember one woman saying that she liked being "enticed" by her husband, when he treated her as the virgin-bride that she was when they came together for the very first time. While men can become excited almost instantaneously, women need to warm up to intimacy by other outward signs of affection. When a man respects this difference and works hard and creatively at producing a romantic and "enticing" situation for the two of them, he usually finds his wife much more responsive to his desires.

Margie: I have heard that some women just don't like sex. Even though they love their husbands and feel obligated to give them

180

What a surprise...! When I saw this, I just thought of you!

their marital rights, if they were to have their preferences, they wouldn't do it at all.

Father JP: It's not uncommon that a young bride complains that she doesn't enjoy sexual intimacy. If she communicates this to her groom, it can make him feel like he is doing wrong or that he is inadequate. Much of it has to do with the fact that the man can satisfy his libido so quickly, whereas a woman needs to time to warm up to intimacy.

Sometimes men are not aware of this difference, thinking that women react as fast as they do. Other times it may be that the man selfishly seeks his own pleasure with no care about his wife's.

Sam: Here we go again, dumping on men. Why are we always the problem?

Father JP: We are not always the problem. Sometimes the man actually does take this difference into account and tries to be sensitive, to warm up his wife with caresses and other acts of affection, which some call "foreplay." But it is the woman who overreacts, thinking that these actions that precede the actual physical union are sinful. Perhaps she reacts this way because the woman lived a chaste and modest adolescence and was taught that such actions are sinful, or lived in a family where this topic wasn't talked about much. If her husband is sensitive, he may also feel guilty because his wife does not seem to enjoy their union, as though he were "using" her.

The two need to realize that the "language of the body" is something good whenever it is oriented toward expressing their spiritual union with union of bodies.

When the couple puts less emphasis on sexual pleasure and intimacy and focuses their efforts on other signs of affection, details of mutual service, taking time to share their feelings, listening to each other without criticizing, then the sexual union comes about more naturally and in a much more satisfying way. Many of the apparent hang-ups of the woman disappear when a man works at making things special for his wife, and he always gets rewarded for it.

Sam: But JP, after a long day of hard work a man is often exhausted and has little or no creative energy left, as you said. Can't a woman understand that? Shouldn't she be satisfied with and appreciate the fact that her husband is working so hard to support her and the kids?

Margie: How can you say that, Sam? Why can't men appreciate how much work goes into caring for the home and the kids?

Father JP: Margie, you get the point that so many of us men often miss. It is true that a man may work very hard at his job to benefit the family, but so does his wife at caring for the home and for the children. When a man helps out even just a little bit with the household chores, it shows his wife that he understands and appreciates how hard she works and how tired she may be. It is much easier for her to respond to his needs when he makes an attempt to respond to hers. However, if her husband only seems to ignore her and her needs, then she feels like "punishing" or getting back at him by ignoring his.

Sam: I never saw it quite like that, but I guess you're right.

Father JP: It is also very important that a man take interest in the kids, because a mother sees her children as an extension of her own being. If her husband seems to be ignoring the kids, she instinctively feels as though he were ignoring her. If he takes an interest in them, she feels as though he was interested in her.

Besides that, as she sees him playing with the kids and having fun with them, it may provoke in her a desire to "play." It actually helps her warm up to him by remembering playful times they had together. It also helps the father get out of himself.

I hope you can see how this mutual respect can help both husband and wife get out of themselves and become better people for each other and for the family. Sam — like a dating couple — you and Margie can already prepare yourselves for a happy marriage by learning to have a greater respect for each other.

In a sense, sexual intercourse can help a man and woman have a greater emotional "unity of life." Everything they do then becomes an emotional unity: work, details of service and affection, care for the children — all is preparation for intimacy and an expression of this total self-giving.

Sam: But if we are not having sex, how do we show that mutual respect and live that "unity of life"?

Father JP: By not trying to take advantage of Margie, you show her that you respect her gift of herself. Through willingness to serve her and take care of her needs before marriage, you show that, once married, you will do precisely the same. Margie, you should respect Sam now while you date, by not provoking or giving in to his sex-drive, but constantly insisting on commitment and service. Giving him a kiss or a hug after signs of commitment and service is more important than your feeling a desire for romance.

Different Fears: Impotence or Loneliness?

Sam: That makes some sense, although I'm not quite convinced. You also say that men and women fear different things. How so?

Father JP: In general, men fear being inadequate, because men are naturally performance and results oriented. Men and women often fear not doing well what they are naturally good at. Men fear being inadequate at school, work, or parenting. In the sexual realm, many men have an underlying fear of not being able to perform or to please a woman sexually. This fear often leads boys to brag about going further with a girl than they actually did.

So to prove themselves "adequate," some young men are tempted to try having sexual relations with someone "safe" — someone who would not be a risk to their male ego. If anyone would stop to think this over, he would see how ridiculous it was. But this is one of those fears that a man would never reveal, since just having such fear manifests inadequacy and great weakness.

Sam: Some of the guys I know think that women judge us men on our "performance" in bed. So these men constantly compare notes in order to find ways to improve that performance.

Margie: Too bad they don't realize women care less about passion and are more driven by romance. The thought of a romantic experience is much more exciting to us than a mere sexual one.

Sam: I think I'm beginning to understand that.

Father JP: I think you're beginning to get it.

Another fear that men have is commitment. This is especially true today, when there is so much pain and anguish associated with divorce, especially for children. If a man has experienced this firsthand as a child, then the fear can be quite great.

Men fear sacrifice and pain while they try to maximize their fun and pleasure. We can get over this fear with a chain of accomplishments. A man may decide to "try out" a woman to see whether she is a serious risk for sacrifice, that is, whether a relationship with her will entail hardship, demands that he can't handle, or nagging, for example. He may also want to know how well she can "perform" to meet his sexual appetites. So many men suggest to their girlfriends to live together prior to marriage: "Let's try it out before we make a lifetime commitment. We don't want to make a mistake." Although this goes against a woman's natural instinct for security, unfortunately some women are weak and agree to such arrangements. Perhaps these women fear that no one else would ever love them enough to marry them, so they'd better stick with this one, and they end up going along with the man's suggestion.

But as we saw earlier, these arrangements don't work. They are based on fear of commitment instead of mutual trust and respect. This shows up in statistical studies: 40 percent of couples who live together break up before marriage, and those who do marry have a 50 percent greater chance of divorce than couples who live apart until marriage.[24] That means that less than 30 percent of living-together couples continue in a lasting marital commitment.

Sam: But JP, let's face it, many people think it is better to try things out before marriage, just as you would take a car for a test drive before buying it. Everybody wants to minimize the risk of buying a lemon. Why can't we do the same with trying to find the right marriage partner?

Father JP: In marriage, you are not purchasing a sex partner. That's prostitution. Marriage is a mutual gift of one's total self. True love always involves risk and sacrifice. One can minimize the risk by really getting to know the other person's personality, likes and dislikes, life values, religious beliefs, and so on. One does not minimize risk by physical intimacy, rather one increases that risk.

What if someone said, let's try out death? Let's try life in a different context, like growing up in another family or in another period of history.

185

Sam: That's ridiculous — and impossible.

Father JP: So it is with love.

Margie: Father JP, although women don't fear commitment as much as men do, we seem to fear inadequacy just as much as men do.

Father JP: Margie, men fear what women seek in a relationship: commitment. But, as you say, women fear being inadequate, but in a different way. What women fear most is being unlovable and unwanted. Not to be loved and to remain alone is the greatest failure in a woman's eyes. A woman feels vulnerable when she senses that no one really loves her. That is why it is important to have other people in your life who love you. Not being on good terms with your parents or with your brothers and sisters or at least with some good, close friends, makes women prime targets for being used by a man.

This fear extends to the physical realm too. A woman fears being unattractive, especially to her man. There is a natural longing to be physically attractive to men, to be desired by them. Women often compare their physical attractiveness and charm with other women because of this fear. Sometimes this may lead a woman to "give in" to a man's desires, because if a guy gets physical with her then she thinks it means that he is attracted to her. However, this may leave her empty, thinking that her physical beauty is the only valuable quality she has. And again, if another more attractive woman comes along to "replace" her in a man's pleasure-seeking eyes, then all her sense of value and self-worth is destroyed.

Margie: Women also fear that their biological clock is ticking and that their opportunity to get married and have children is passing them by.

Father JP: Yes. They also fear that they may miss the opportunity to be loved and wanted by children. This too can cause women to choose men in an act of desperation rather than searching out the man who would make a loving husband and a good father.

Women do have a notable feminine quality that gives them a greater natural capacity for sympathy, for putting themselves in the shoes of others and for identifying with the needs and feelings of others as their own. Thus, if a woman sees a hungry child, she will instinctively respond by feeding the child despite her own hunger, tiredness, or illness. Likewise, when a woman sees a grieving person, she naturally grieves along with him. Men are not so naturally inclined, but tend to fill their own desires first and tend to look for solutions to the problems of others rather than to console them and sympathize with them.

Sam: Hey, you're knocking us men again while pointing out only the good qualities of women. Let's be fair.

Father JP: Don't worry, Sam. These natural feminine qualities can become a woman's greatest weakness. A woman can selfishly turn this "sympathizing" toward herself. If so, she ends up projecting her own feelings onto another person. A woman can jump to conclusions. For example, she'll tell herself, "Jack didn't call me at the usual time. That means he doesn't love me." She does this because she thinks that the only way she would ever miss calling Jack at the usual time would be because she didn't love him anymore. She "sympathizes" with herself, projecting her own potential feelings onto her boyfriend.

Sam: JP, that is so true. You hit that nail on the head. How many arguments have arisen because Margie assumed I had bad intentions when I did or said something?

Father JP: Well, this can severely affect a relationship. For example, a woman may think: "The only way I could ever get intimate with Mr. X would be if I really loved him and were committed to this relationship. Therefore, if he decides to become physically intimate with me, then it must be because he loves me and is committed to me."

Another bad situation would be if a woman feared she was unlovable and unattractive in addition to her being a selfish "sympathizer." Perhaps she is convinced that no one else would ever want her. Such a woman — even if she was a very good and deeply religious woman — is set up to compromise her core values. I have repeatedly seen good women — women who had strong convictions that sexual relations before marriage were wrong — give in and end up in very sad situations.

Margie: That hasn't happened with me and Sam, but I can see how it could happen.

Father JP: It is good to keep in mind the power of temptation and how men and women think differently.

Margie: I agree.

Father JP: Let me give you another example.

When a man becomes tired and stressed out, he usually deals with it by withdrawing into himself. He will become quiet and distance himself from others. He does this to mull over his problems in hope of finding a solution. Maybe he watches TV, plays sports, or just seeks quiet rest. John Gray calls this "finding relief in the cave."

Women think differently. If they have a problem, women try to find relief and to feel understood by talking it out. So, when a woman sees her man in a stressed out, problem-solving mode, she may think he lacks interest in her, that something is wrong with the relationship, and that she may be losing him. When a man is in this removed and unresponsive mode, he makes her feel powerless and insecure, and her natural instinct is to protect the relationship by comforting him, being physically affectionate, and giving him more than is proper.

Margie: Father JP, all this seems to say that a woman's desire to have a secure relationship and her compassionate nature motivate her to compromise and to have inappropriate intimacies with a man. I can see that happening with a man of character, but some women compromise with men who are real jerks. I guess that sometimes women just don't know when to let go.

Ugh, I just need to rest and think...

Father JP: Margie that is so true. Women are opposite to men in this: whereas men fear commitment, women tend to become attached to a man, even when he is bad or abusive. Men can easily hop from one woman to another; it is much harder for a woman to let go after falling for a man.

A woman's tendency to stick with her man can be good, since it can move her to put up with a man's defects for the good of the relationship and for the good of their children. Of course, when lived to the extreme, it can cause a woman to stick by a man who is not good for her or for her future children, such as a man who is alcoholic, abusive, or a womanizer.

We can really be blind. A man's outward signs of affection may disguise his real motivation; he may be only seeking to gratify himself. A woman's "wishful" thinking can get the better of her and fool her into a false sense of security about a relationship. When this is coupled with a fear of losing her man, she sets herself up to be used and abused. She would be much better off if she looked for real signs of love and commitment in the ways that men show them, and she should be ready to leave him immediately — before she becomes attached — if those signs are not there.

Expressing Love Differently

Margie: How do men show love differently from women?

Father JP: Men show love and commitment through steadfastness and sacrifice.

A man can be attracted to a woman simply because of her looks. If another woman comes along who is prettier or who has some other attractive quality, then an uncommitted guy will drop the first and go for the second. But when a man makes certain and ongoing sacrifices to stay with his woman, he shows true love; when he decides to stick with her after she refuses to gratify him sexually, it is a sign that he has true love and commitment.

So, if we have a woman who imagines that men only get physical if they have love and commitment for a woman, and we have a man who will say and do just about anything to gratify his desires, then we have a relationship heading for disaster.

However, if we have a woman who refuses to "sympathize" with herself but insists on true signs of love and commitment, and we have a man who will keep his eyes and heart on one woman, willing to show his love and commitment by making sacrifices — especially that of waiting until marriage — then we have a relationship with a potential to last.

A man also shows his love and steadfastness by being the first to say "I'm sorry" and ask for forgiveness. That is a way to say, "Look, I didn't mean to hurt you. You mean a lot to me. I can't afford to lose you." The man needs to make an almost heroic effort to be understanding, to overlook and excuse a woman's emotional sensitivities and her tendency to project intentions onto him. After listening to her "complaint," he needs to explain his actual intentions and take responsibility for not taking her

All wet for love.

feelings into account. Yet at the same time, he can remind her that she should not project her feelings onto him; men do not always have the same motives as women when they do or say something perceived as hurtful.

A man who does all this really loves his woman.

Sam: So, JP, we men aren't so bad after all.

Father JP: No, we're not. A man will also show his love by being available for his girlfriend. That is, he is ready to drop everything to attend to her needs and wishes. If a man will stop his work or stop watching a very exciting football game in order to attend to his girlfriend's needs, then she knows he really loves her.

Sam: JP, you're upping the ante here. Are there ways that a man can tell whether a woman has true love for him?

Father JP: I guess you want me to take some of the pressure off you, eh, Sam?

Well, women do show love in different ways than men. When a woman really loves a man, she will have a deep-seated faith in him. She will have faith that he will be able to do what is necessary to bring the relationship and family ahead despite all obstacles. A woman who criticizes her man and second-guesses his decisions lacks true feminine love.

Actually, a man can take criticism from just about anybody except two people in his life. Who do you think those people are?

Margie: His mother and his wife?

Father JP: You got it! A man cannot take criticism from either his mother or his wife. If it comes from a girlfriend, then he can always dump her.

Growing up, if a boy's mother criticizes him he thinks, "Wow! She must be right because she knows me more than I know myself." If another man criticizes him, he sees that as a challenge and it motivates him to prove the other wrong.

When a man marries, his wife assumes the maternal role in his eyes. If a man is unemployed or going through some other trial, the last thing he needs is to hear that he is useless and good for nothing. And when a woman criticizes her husband for being a bad father for not spending more time with the kids, then he thinks she must be right, so why even try.

So, a woman will show her faith and love by being always very encouraging, looking for ways to motivate her man to excel. If a man does not improve in his studies or profession after falling in love with a woman, it is questionable how sincere and selfless their love really is for each other. Perhaps the man is escaping from the pressures of his studies by spending time with his girlfriend and pleasing her. A good girlfriend would temper her own desire to be with her boyfriend and encourage him to do what he needs to do to excel.

192

You are my inspiration... I knew you could do it!

Margie: Women don't like to be criticized either. Shouldn't men be careful not to criticize us?

Father JP: True, men should also avoid criticism. However, when a man criticizes, he often doesn't mean it. He is just passing the blame for his own failure (which he can't face at the moment) onto someone else. So a woman would do well not to take men seriously when they criticize or joke about her defects. Nevertheless, if they really want to grow in their relationship, neither women nor men ought to criticize.

Margie, because of your feminine tendency to project motives and feelings onto others, you will naturally take offense at things that Sam will say and do, assuming that he must have the same motives and feelings you would have if you were to say or do the same to him. Explain these feelings to Sam, but at the same time listen to Sam and let him explain his true motives and meaning. Respect and trust what he tells you even though it may be hard. Whatever you do, avoid critical and cynical remarks, which men will naturally take as implying that they are inadequate. This may seem one-sided, but it is good "feminine psychology."

Sam: Everything you've said rings true, but what can I do to help Margie avoid those feminine weaknesses? It seems like this just has to happen on its own, which means for us that we have an almost impossible task before us.

Father JP: Sam, keep in mind that a man's weakness is complemented by a woman's strength and a woman's weakness is complemented by a man's strength. Men and women are different. For example, you can help Margie out by reassuring her that she is attractive to you without getting overly physical. If she asks you to compare her to another woman, remind her how unique she is and that her outer beauty only makes her inner beauty shine. Tell her that there is no competition and that you would never want to focus on another woman's physical attributes in order to reassure her of how attractive she is to you and how much you love her.

You should also try to foster Margie's faith in you, reminding her of the things that you have done that truly show your love, despite having let her down at other times. Work at ways that show her that you are worthy of her trust — for instance, showing her that you don't trust yourself too much by not putting you and her in situations in which you could offend her and God. Show her that you take precautions with other women because you don't want to risk damaging your relationship with her. Good priests certainly take such precautions because they don't trust themselves.

Sam: Sometimes when Margie says "no" I feel offended. It seems that her refusals are a rejection of me and they make me feel lonely.

Margie: Then Sam makes me feel guilty for not giving him what he wants.

Father JP: Margie, you need to reassure Sam that your refusal to give in is not a rejection of him as a person or as a man but a self-defense mechanism to preserve this gift of yourself for that very special moment of your wedding day. Should the two of you choose to make that commitment, then those more intimate physical signs of love will be appropriate and will reflect and reinforce the meaning of a complete and total commitment that you will then have. You can remind him that this is something that both of you have decided and is what you want for each other.

Sam, try to avoid putting Margie on the spot. Try to respect her as you would a sister. When she reproves you, take it as a love tap from someone who wants the best for you. It is a reminder that she wants you to experience what it is like to go into marriage with a pure heart and with a body unselfishly oriented toward one person. She is really doing this for your own good and because she really loves you.

Margie, you can help Sam out a lot by being aware of how easily his sensuality is triggered and by avoiding that. Outward signs of affection are good, but they should not be prolonged or provocative. Respect the strong and constant sex drive that God has given him. Remind Sam how well he "performs" those true manly ways of showing love: service, sacrifice, and fidelity. Tell him how much you appreciate it when he opens the door for you, when he compliments you, when he gets up to serve you something at a meal, when he volunteers to wash the dishes for your mother. These are the signs of true love that you look for.

If both of you work at this, you will learn valuable communication skills as well as help Margie avoid the temptation to seek that assurance of commitment by physical intimacy.

Margie: So Sam must carry some of the load of avoiding sexual intimacy too. Most people seem to think that this is exclusively the woman's responsibility.

Father JP: It is hard to do it alone. Falling in love and deepening that love is a team effort. It is part of the challenge and fun of dating.

Margie: What about when Sam goes into one of his quiet "cave" modes?

Father JP: Sam, when you get stressed out and tired, try to re-assure Margie that you love her and that it is not a reflection on your relationship, that you need "space" to figure things out.

Margie, be patient with Sam. Sometimes you can share silent moments together; other times you can just let him do his things, trusting that he will come out of his "cave" with greater eagerness to give himself to you.

Sam: JP, you were talking about reassuring Margie that there is no competition. One thing that bugs me is that sometimes she gets all upset when I have lunch with an old friend of mine from high school, a friend who happens to be a woman. I try to reassure Margie that there is nothing between us, that we are just old friends, but that doesn't go very far with her.

Father JP: Sam, as you and Margie get closer and spend more time together, things are bound to change, especially in your re-lationships with others. What you do with other women is going to affect the relationship between the two of you. That's natural.

One way to look at it is, that as the two of you get closer and become more and more *one,* then your personal relationship to a particular person must become a joint relation of you and Margie to that person. Thus, if Margie does not feel comfortable with the relationship, then it means that the two of you are not comfortable with the relationship. You have to find ways to make outside relationships bring you closer together or else they will eventually pull you apart.

This also means that relationships with people of the opposite sex are going to become more distant and less familiar as your relationship with Margie becomes more exclusive.

Certainly you want to make sure to avoid sharing intimate details of your life and relationship with Margie with any other woman.

Sam: Well, what about sharing details with your same-sex friends? Not that this is a problem with me, but women seem to be pretty free in sharing those kinds of things with each other. Just listen in to some office chatter sometime — it can be pretty ugly.

Father JP: It is a great advantage to maintain and deepen your friendship with same-sex friends while dating. Since women don't really connect with the guy-stuff that you like to do, Sam, then you will benefit from finding another outlet for that besides Margie, no matter how understanding and accommodating she becomes. Likewise, Margie you need an outlet for your woman-to-woman stuff, although within limits. Just as it would be bad for Sam to get together with guys to analyze female anatomy, similarly it is bad for women to get together to analyze intimate details of people and relationships. For Sam to spend time with the guys — or you, Margie, with your girlfriends — will help each of you keep perspective on your relationship.

It is especially helpful to get to know other young couples — ones who share similar values — to do things with together. Those couples become a great support group. You can help one another. And if you have a particular difficulty or concern, you can discuss it with that friend — man-to-man or woman-to-woman — who can help you put perspective on the issue in question.

Margie: That makes sense, Father JP, and I know a couple that I think would be a great support for us.

Father JP: Also, Sam and Margie, if you want to save yourselves for marriage, you have to make sure to avoid certain shows or types of dancing that are provocative or even downright erotic. But I think the two of you are already in tune with this.

Sam: Yes, JP, I think we're getting the point. Thanks for the advice and insights that you have given both of us. It wasn't what I expected when I came here to talk. I really expected to expose gaping holes in the Catholic teachings. I have a lot more respect for them now — and you are right, they are very much in the same line as ancient Jewish teachings. We have a lot in common.

197

Father JP: Sam, you are a very noble guy. It takes guts to come in here and talk to a priest of another religion, especially of a religion that our society and the media consider medieval and arcane. I have enjoyed these conversations and hope they have helped. I have certainly learned a lot from your questions; they have forced me to think.

Sam: JP, you've deepened my understanding of love and human sexuality. I am still trying to put it all together. Thanks for taking this time with us.

Father JP: If you have more questions, don't be afraid to come back. I look forward to the opportunities to discuss these questions or others that may come up.

Margie: Thank you, Father.

Father JP: You're welcome. Like I said, I have benefited greatly from these conversations myself. Thank you!

Vocation:
What Does God Want of Me?

Although the joint conversations between Margie, Sam, and Father JP ended there, Margie continued going to confession and seeking advice from Father JP. Certainly she was happy that things were more under control in her relationship with Sam. The two of them had been talking more and more about the possibility of marriage, yet the question of her vocation kept nagging Margie, which had been on her mind off and on in the past. For some reason, this matter still bothered her and now she felt the need to discuss it with Father JP.

Do I Have a Vocation?

Margie: Hi, Father JP, it's me again. Thank you again for hearing my confession. Do you have time for a few questions?

Father JP: Sure, Margie, go right ahead.

Margie: I still find it hard to say "no" to Sam's advances. Although he doesn't take those noes as a personal rejection as much, he still complains a bit.

Father JP: That's the way it will be until the day you marry; its part of that constant male sex-drive. Be constant and firm while remaining understanding. Men also have a very logical mind that can rationalize just about anything, so when it gets mixed in with their sexual emotion, it does no good to argue or reason with them. The only logic that men really understand in this situation is simply NO!

Remember, until a woman teaches her man to be a father, he basically remains a little boy who wants his instant gratification. Your saying "no" to him helps him make that transition.

Margie: I guess you're right. I just feel sorry for him in those moments. Oh, there's my feminine weakness getting the best of me.

Father JP: You're starting to get it!

Margie: I guess so.

By the way, well, I don't know quite how to say this. It is something that has been in the back of my mind for some time. Well, I wonder if I might have a vocation.

Father JP: Of course you do! All of us Christians have a vocation.

Margie: What?

Father JP: Yes, God gives each Christian a vocation.

Margie: I think you did mention that before, but I didn't quite make sense of it all. You are not saying that God wants everyone to become priests or nuns, are you?

Father JP: No, not at all. God calls all Christians to become saints and to strive for perfection. We are all called to see Jesus Christ in the needs of those around us and to serve Him there. Some of us are called to do this in a vocation of lifetime celibacy while others receive a vocation to marriage; each must strive for holiness and serve Christ where He calls us.

Tell me, Margie, what makes you think that you might have a vocation to be a nun? That is what you were referring to, wasn't it, when you said that you thought you might have a vocation?

Margie: I've been thinking and praying about what you said in our last meeting. Sam and I have been discussing the different topics you suggested and we have had some very deep talks. More and more the idea of marrying Sam appeals to me. But I was thinking about something that one of my teachers said

Wouldn't it have been easier if...?

to me in high school, that I'd make a good nun. At the time I thought she was crazy, but now I wonder whether or not she might be right. If God is calling me, I just want to make sure that I am not running away from Him. How do I know?

Father JP: Vocation is a very personal thing and is different for each person. Generically, we say that each one has a vocation to strive for holiness and to serve Christ in the Church and in his fellow man. A vocation is not just a *task* that God assigns to accomplish in this life. A vocation is a call to love Him in a very particular way, to become partners with Him in a wonderful adventure of love. A vocation is a special gift that God gives to each one individually and to no one else, but He wants us to use it to serve others.

Something similar happens with our talents and work: we are all called to support ourselves and do something for the common good of society through some kind of work. But not everyone is called to do the same type of work. Some will be engineers, others bus drivers or teachers. Each one of us is given a unique set of talents and gifts to use in concert with others for the greater good of mankind.

Each person must discern the particular way God wants him or her to strive for holiness and serve Him, just as each person must discern his or her particular professional career or vocation. In fact, our profession is actually an important dimension of our vocation from God.

How Do I Discern My Vocation?

Margie: That seems to be my dilemma. How do I discern my particular vocation?

Father JP: Our personal vocation is a freely given gift from God that involves His personal and unrepeatable invitation: *I have called you by your name, you are mine* (Isaiah 43:1). In this sense, our personal vocation is more than just a job, because it guides us into a particular and unique relationship with God and invites us to participate in making Christ known to others in a singular way. This invitation may first appear as a desire to do something great and to make a difference in the world. Our life seems empty just doing what we are doing, pursuing selfish aims. This desire moves us to be better and to search for the path for which God has destined us — the path that will give full meaning to our lives through our self-gift.

We normally don't hear that call through some kind of audible voice. We discover it by discerning the particular talents with which God has gifted us. If we are poor at math, then God is probably not calling us to become engineers. Thus, through learning, trial and error, and study we learn what abilities we do or do not have. God may speak to me through the gifts He gives me; I listen to Him by discovering that I am not good at math or science, but instead I have the talent for learning languages.

Next, God calls us to use our talents to serve Him in others. To discern His call, we need to consider what opportunities and societal needs exist that fit our gifts and talents. I may be a decent piano player, but since there are very few positions available for concert pianists, then that is less likely to be my professional career. Perhaps I could use my gift for languages to become a translator, or use it along with my musical ability to become a teacher of music and languages in a high school; or maybe I must use and develop other talents altogether.

Margie: Besides my talent for English literature and history, I think that I am good with kids. That's why I enjoy teaching fourth graders. However, I can also see myself devoting all my energies to being a mother.

Father JP: Discerning our vocation is like putting pieces of a puzzle together; discovering our talents puts just one or two of the pieces in place. Our talents may make us adequate to fill many different positions and, of course, just because our talents happen to match the requirements of a specific position doesn't mean that it is necessarily our calling. Other pieces of the puzzle include the person doing the hiring who may decide to choose someone else for that position, even though you are well qualified. So God also uses human choices in communicating our religious and professional vocation to us. If Sam does not ask you to marry him, then forming a family with him will not be God's will for you. Likewise, if, for example, the Carmelites decide that you do not fit into their community, then that too is not for you.

Your choice is also important. Even if Sam were to ask you to marry him, you may discern that the difference in religi . and other factors disqualifies him as a candidate. Or after visiting the Carmelite community, they decide you are a suitable aspirant for their order, but you do not see yourself fitting into that way of life, then you are free to choose not to go. Even if you did see Sam as a suitable candidate or even if you did see yourself fitting into the Carmelite community, God wants you to freely choose to answer His call.

Thus, God calls us through the gifts He gives us and in the needs of others, respecting and using the free will of all the individuals involved.

Margie: But I am a little afraid of my freedom — that I might make a decision that I'll regret later. How can I discern my true vocation?

Father JP: Margie, there are several things you can do. The first and most important is to develop your life of prayer, especially asking that God help you see His plan for you. Even if your vocation is to marriage, prayer can help you find and be sure that you are marrying the right person and for the right reason. Even after we begin to follow our particular path, we need prayer to sustain and guide us along the way. We can complement our prayer with the reading of Scripture, especially the Gospels. God communicates to us through His Word. But don't read the Gospels like a newspaper or history book — to get some information about God. Read it like a love letter, which never gets old and which you can read over and over again to receive new insights into God and your relationship with Him. Also, spend time in front of the Eucharist and attend Holy Mass more frequently; there is nothing like "getting intimate" with Christ to discover His will for you. Specifically, you should ask Him about His vocational plan for you.

Margie: My prayer life has improved quite a bit since I came back to the Church, but I guess there is still room for improvement. Often my prayer is kind of hit or miss.

Father JP: Try coming more regularly to talk and discuss these matters. In fact, this is what the Church calls "spiritual direction." The Catholic Church has always recommended spiritual direction for those striving for sanctity. It should be seen as a kind of conversation with an older brother or sister, with an experienced friend or father. A spiritual director is a kind of "coach" in the area of our spiritual life and our Christian witness to others.

Spiritual direction will help you be more accountable for your prayer life as well as help you in your discernment. If you find it hard to come here, you can get spiritual direction or guidance with some trustworthy person, one who is a prayerful soul and who has a good knowledge of the Faith. Bouncing our ideas, desires, and fears off another person helps us to be objective, so that we don't just seek some excuse to hide from God and flee His call, like Jonah did in the Old Testament.

We also want to make sure we are not leaving out some important factor in our decision making that we may have over-looked because of our inexperience. We can benefit from a director's experience and knowledge, not to mention from his prayers for us. If you choose a laywoman or religious nun, she can do much to help you in your vocational discovery; however, it is also good to confer with a good priest from time to time. The Sacrament of Confession complements spiritual direction by helping us eliminate the spiritual obstacles to following our vocation.

Margie: I can see how that will help. By the way, you are one of the few priests I know who gives spiritual direction. Other priests seem too busy. What is one to do if she cannot find a priest who gives spiritual direction?

Father JP: It is true that many priests do not feel that they are prepared or have the time for this ministry. But if you need to find a priest for spiritual direction, don't get discouraged. You can always ask your local priest to recommend a priest with sound judgment who does offer spiritual direction. You may also try asking him if he has any particular concerns about a decision that you are considering or about advice that you have received.

Margie: So prayer life and spiritual direction: is that all I need to discern my vocation?

Father JP: A third thing, if you feel God is calling you in a particular direction: it is important to know what that vocation involves. If a person feels drawn to marriage, one learns about this vocation just by experiencing the way Mom and Dad interact. However, if one grows up in a dysfunctional family, then one should spend time with mentoring couples that have a good family life, just to learn what the trials of a good marriage are and how each person deals with those trials differently. If you feel a possible call to the Daughters of Charity, then you should spend time with them. This information is helpful to learn whether you fit with them and they with you.

Fourth, after praying, asking advice, and gathering information, one must be willing to take the risk and simply decide.

Margie: While growing up, I was told that the vocation to the priesthood or the religious life is the ideal for a Catholic.

Father JP: The vocation to the priesthood and religious life is a great ideal, but it is not for everybody. It depends on God and His will for you.

If you had a vocation to the religious life, but said "no," you would always have regrets about not following Our Lord when He called. However, the same would be true if you had met the right man and were called to a vocation of marriage with him but ended up saying "no" to enter the religious life instead. Our vocation is not only a gift but also a mission; we will be happy in this life and bear much fruit — and God will be happy with us — if we strive to be generous and please Him with our lives in an unselfish manner, whatever our vocation may be.

Margie: Father JP, do you know anyone who got married, realizing that they were saying "no" to Our Lord? Did they regret it afterward?

Father JP: Yes, Margie, I do know individuals who were in this situation. Usually it happens after they had received a clear calling and made a commitment to Christ. Later, because of temptations of the flesh, loneliness, or personal differences with others, they chose to abandon their commitments. Only later, after the emotions died down, did they realize their mistake. Some admit their mistake, regret it, and would undo it if they had the power to do so. Others deny their mistake, blaming others for not persevering in their vocation and virginal commitments to Our Lord.

Margie: What about the other way around, are there celibate men and women who regret their decision?

Father JP: Yes, it happens. Usually those who make a mistake in committing themselves to Christ in a virginal way discover this in a matter of months or within a few years of making this decision. The Church always makes sure that one cannot make such a lifelong commitment until they have actually lived with this decision for five to ten years. Perhaps such people discover that they cannot fully give themselves. This is often accompanied by a deep and ongoing feeling of emptiness or loss at the thought of living the rest of one's life without a partner and without the possibility of having children.

One has to be cautious here, however, because almost every celibate man or woman is tempted by this thought at some point in his or her calling. But when it is a persistent and enduring disposition, and when it is not attached to other external factors such as selfishness, imprudence, and interpersonal difficulties, then it may be a sign that one has not properly discerned one's calling.

Actually the same can happen the other way around. I have known individuals engaged to be married who felt a deep and enduring emptiness, that somehow that was not enough for them, that their lives would be incomplete if they did not give it all to God. How courageous they were to cancel their wedding plans in order to pursue a celibate vocation.

Margie: Then I guess it would be a very serious sin not to follow your calling?

Father JP: Margie, not following one's vocation is not a sin in the same sense as something like murder would be. Murder, fornication, and stealing go against God's will and commandments that apply to everyone without exception.

Choosing to follow one's vocation involves many factors. Some people may see their vocation clearly and say "no." If

Wouldn't it have been easier if...?

they were to do this to spite God, then certainly sin would be involved. Others only vaguely see their vocation and have a hard time saying "yes." There may be emotional factors, family pressures, and other such things that obscure the decision-making process. Still others only discover and develop a relationship with God later in life after marriage has already taken place. The main thing is that each one should strive to be generous, to listen attentively to God's voice, and strive to please Him in everything.

Margie: Wouldn't it be more generous and pleasing to God to remain a virgin?

Father JP: Virginity is certainly one way to live generosity with God, but it is not the only way.

Motherhood and fatherhood can bring out the virtue of generosity in a woman or man who is not prepared for the generosity of a virginal commitment. Worldly attachments and unbridled passions may have such a strong hold on such a person that they may keep him or her from being truly generous. Parenthood can bring out a pure, self-sacrificing love in such a man or woman. When he or she must get up in the middle of the night to feed a child or change a diaper, when the couple has to opt for more modest vacations or drop plans for buying that favorite sports car — all because of the children they brought into the world — then they may learn what generosity is by living it. As the *Catechism of the Catholic Church* puts it:

> *After the fall, marriage helps [one] overcome self-absorption, egoism, pursuit of one's own pleasure, and to open oneself to the other, to mutual aid and to self-giving.* (CCC 1609)

Marriage itself contains a call for a man and a woman to get out of themselves, to transcend the boundaries of self-interest, and to seek to the good of someone else. It is a kind of losing of self, a sacrifice of self, that enables each to become more truly and completely him- or herself.

Margie: But what about all the good that a woman could do for the Church if she would remain a virgin?

Father JP: Virginity is certainly one very good way to serve God and the Church. However, a married couple carries out a wonderful apostolate when they generously give themselves to each other, when they receive each child as a true gift from God, and when they spend themselves in raising their children in virtue and in faith. They can give a marvelous witness to others since they ought to love one another as Christ loved the Church and gave himself for her by pouring out His Blood on the Cross (Ephesians 5:25–32). When others see that kind of love in a couple, they want to be part of it; they long for the same kind of love; they are drawn toward the family and toward the source of that love, God. Besides, the family is a "domestic Church," the place where good parents teach their children to become virtuous men and women who will become the future leaders for the Church and society. It has been said that we have few good priestly vocations because we have few good families, which are the seedbeds of priestly and religious vocations. The vocation to marriage may entail great sacrifices, but also it entails the possibility of reaping great fruit.

Margie: If marriage is such a beautiful and fruitful thing, then why doesn't the Church let priests marry?

Father JP: Celibacy is a gift with a twofold purpose: one is to be available to dedicate oneself to God's things, and the other is to witness to the virginal love that the Church has for Christ and Christ for the Church. In marriage, one is called to serve God by generously giving oneself to one's spouse and children. After doing that, most people have little time or energy to serve the needs of anyone else. But a person who lives a celibate life has more time and energy to dedicate to God, the Church, and the needy. St. Paul mentions this:

> *I wish that all were as I myself am. But each has his own special gift from God, one of one kind and one of*

another....I want you to be free from anxieties. The un-married man is anxious about the affairs of the Lord, how to please the Lord; but the married man is anxious about worldly affairs, how to please his wife. (1 Corinthians 7:7, 32–33)

If priests married, they wouldn't have as much time and energy to dedicate themselves to God's family.

Margie: Isn't this view of celibacy somewhat utilitarian?

Father JP: It could be, Margie, you're right. However, just like marriage is more than just a "useful" institution for raising children, so celibacy means more than just availability to serve.

You could think of it this way, comparing it to the two sisters of Lazarus, Martha and Mary. Mary chose to put herself at the feet of Our Lord, to dedicate her full attention to Him, while Martha was busy taking care of the normal household tasks of a wife and mother. When Martha complained, Our Lord said:

Martha, Martha, you are anxious and troubled about many things; one thing is needful. Mary has chosen the good portion, which shall not be taken away from her. (Luke 10:41–42)

Mary — like the celibate person — can more easily put all her time and energy into being attentive to Our Lord. The married man or woman may indeed serve Christ in serving family needs, but it is harder to focus directly on the things of God.

Moreover, married love is a kind of sign and sacrament of the mutual love between Christ and the Church,[25] whereas, virginity is a kind of sign and sacrament of the innocence of Christ's bride and of the pure virginal love that she ought to have for Him — a total and complete love:

You shall love the Lord your God with all your heart, and with all your soul, and with all your mind, and with all your strength. (Mark 12:30)

211

Religious life has many different forms. Some orders are principally dedicated to prayer and devotion to Christ their spouse, whereas others are quite active in some external apostolate, such as teaching Christ in children or caring for Christ in the sick. An essential aspect of religious life is becoming "living martyrs" who remind all mankind that we are not living for this world but for the next. The evangelical counsels — chastity, poverty, and obedience — exemplify the sacrificial character of this witness: chastity, foregoing marital pleasures for the bliss of heaven; poverty, foregoing worldly riches for a heavenly treasure; obedience, subjecting oneself to the will of one's spouse, Christ. In a sense, voluntary virginity or celibacy "for the kingdom" is a sign and anticipation of heaven, of the resurrection when we will "neither marry nor be given in marriage, but will be like angels in heaven" (Mark 12:25).

Men are called to the priesthood to share in a special way in the paternity of Christ, becoming a kind of sacrament of Christ's love for the Church. Their call to celibacy makes them available for the needs of God's family, the Church, and identifies them more fully with the chaste way Christ lived His life on behalf of His bride, the Church. He who feels called to the priesthood must have a big heart and the desire to understand and forgive the most horrible crimes that a person could possibly commit. He must also have a great love for the Holy Mass and the desire to bring the Eucharist to others.

Margie: What about my Aunt Cory? She never married nor did she become a nun, although she is quite devout. Is celibacy part of her Christian vocation?

Father JP: Did she do anything special with her extra time and availability?

Margie: She took wonderful care of her ailing father for many years.

Father JP: Laymen and laywomen may be called to live a celibate life in the middle of the world in order to be available to serve others and the Church. In this way, they become a kind

212

of sacrament of the maternal love of the Church, like a mother who is constantly looking out for the needs of her children, especially the most needy. Sometimes one makes the choice to remain celibate to meet particular needs of a parent, sibling, or other family member. Others choose to do so in order to help meet certain needs of society or apostolic needs of the Church.

For example, those called to Opus Dei — which includes celibate and married men and women; priests and laity — have a special apostolic mission to spread the awareness of the universal call to holiness, providing ordinary Catholics with the means to reach such holiness, such as providing them spiritual direction and Christian formation. All who receive a vocation to Opus Dei realize they have received a very special grace and they correspond to that gift by striving to sanctify themselves through their everyday work and through carrying out their family and social duties. Those who live celibacy in Opus Dei are more available to provide spiritual and apostolic "coaching" and Christian formation to others, but that is part of the mission of every member of Opus Dei.

All these different vocations are needed for the Church to carry out her mission to be light and salt to the world. Do you feel any particular attraction to one of these paths?

Should I Become a Nun?

Margie: All the various vocations have their particular attraction. I would really like to know which one would be best for me. It seems you're saying that marriage is good, but virginity is better. Is that correct?

Father JP: That's more or less what St. Paul himself said:

> So that he who marries his betrothed does well; and he who refrains from marriage will do better. (1 Corinthians 7:38)

Also, Our Lord more or less said the same thing to Martha, "Mary has chosen the better part" (Luke 10:42).

Margie: Does that mean that I will become holier if I remain a virgin?

Father JP: Let's look at this another way. Both the vocation to marriage and to celibacy are gifts. Objectively speaking, the vocation to celibacy is considered a greater gift because it is oriented toward a greater participation in Christ's mission; it enables one to affect more people through a more universal service to others. However, the gift of celibacy is not given to everyone. We have to learn to love and be grateful for the gifts God gives us. Let's learn to appreciate those gifts and look for ways to use them to serve others and not worry or be envious of what others have been given. Both gifts call us to love God through the service to others.

The degree of holiness depends on the level of one's charity, that is, how much love for God one achieves. Someone who dedicates her virginity to Christ but lacks generosity in her self-giving may not achieve as great a union with Christ as a married man or woman who generously pours him- or herself out for the family out of love of God. That is why each person must discover his or her calling and work at being generous in response.

What would elicit a greater generosity from you, Margie, marriage or becoming and remaining a virgin for love of Christ and his Church?

Margie: I don't know, Father JP. I look at my sinful past and I think that I am unworthy to become a nun.

Father JP: None of us is ever worthy of any vocation. It is a gift that comes from God. You can never earn someone else's love; it must be freely given.

As for your past, look at St. Paul who persecuted the early Church, helped martyr Saint Steven, and put Christians in jail. Yet Our Lord called him. And there is St. Augustine, who was weak in the flesh and even fathered a child by a live-in girlfriend. Yet Our Lord called him to be bishop and one of the greatest theologians and saints in the history of the Church.

However, when considering a particular vocation, we should not ignore our past completely. If our past weaknesses — physical, psychological, or moral — are not completely healed, then they may incline us to future sin and scandal for others. If so, then we'd be better off waiting to prove to ourselves and to those directing us that we can handle the potential demands that come with this vocation.

Margie: On the one hand, consecrated virginity is attractive because it seems to be a greater calling than marriage. Yet, on the other hand, I do picture myself married and having children; that too is a very attractive prospect. Besides, the idea of going a lifetime without someone to love, someone to share the good times and bad, to be there for me when I need him, someone to hold on to when I am down — that seems to be a great and heroic sacrifice, too much for me.

Father JP: Each vocation entails sacrifice. Those called to celibacy and virginity receive a special grace to love God completely and live out this special commitment. But those called to marriage also receive a special grace, the grace to love Christ in and through a very imperfect person, putting up with his or her many faults. They receive the grace to sacrifice themselves for their children, to get up late at night to care for a sick child, and to endure the rebelliousness of their children's teen years. Which takes more sacrifice? I think that most celibate persons would agree that for them marriage would be the greater sacrifice, even though they may have been quite attracted to marriage when they answered God's call to celibacy.

Our Lord calls us to follow Him by embracing sacrifice: "If any man would come after me, let him deny himself and take up his cross daily and follow me" (Luke 9:23). Of course, to choose a vocation (whether to celibacy or to marriage) as a way to run away from the Cross would be selfishly wrong. Nevertheless, to choose a vocation that would be a source of constant complaints and self-pity would be foolish too, for "God loves a cheerful giver" (2 Corinthians 9:7).

Jesus, this is for you!

With that said, I don't want you to think that remaining celibate is all about sacrifice. When God calls a person to sacrifice having a husband or wife, to sacrifice the possibility of having children, he promises to give that person spiritual love and spiritual children that bring a joy and fulfillment that far surpasses any that a natural family could deliver. As Our Lord said to Peter, "Everyone who has left houses or brothers or sisters or father or mother or children or lands, for my name's sake, will receive a hundredfold, and inherit eternal life" (Matthew 19:29).

Margie: So in responding to a vocation, it's not enough to have a particular attraction to one over another?

Father JP: Correct. The particular attraction may be a significant factor in hearing the call, but it does not encompass the whole picture. To see this better, let's return to the analogy of a professional vocation.

In choosing a career, we need to discern and develop our true talents. If I were asked to do a drawing of an eagle, it would take

216

me all day and it would still turn out poorly. I could work and improve my drawing skills, but it would always be a chore for me because my heart would not be in it. However, if you gave me a good philosophy book, I would find it absorbing and could discuss it for hours, even to the point of forgetting to eat. So we need to discover these talents and develop them if we want to be fulfilled in life.

In discerning and choosing a religious or professional vocation, it is not enough to have a capacity to do it. We have to be able to put our heart into it.

Margie: But that approach seems a little selfish to me: to choose a vocation just because one enjoys it.

Father JP: Enjoyment and fulfillment is not the only reason to choose a profession or vocation, but it is important. For example, you wouldn't recommend marrying someone you didn't like, someone who was a chore and a bore to live with, would you?

Margie: No, of course not.

Father JP: The same with a religious or professional vocation. Still there are other factors.

For instance, a man may choose to develop his artistic talent and become a professional artist because he is good at it and enjoys it. But at some point, other factors may affect and change his decision. Perhaps he decides to marry and have children, which may mean that he demotes his artistic pursuits to a vocation or hobby and chooses to work at something else that would provide the financial needs of his new family. Or perhaps he finds teaching art to inner-city kids very rewarding because it helps them become motivated to stay in school and get the education they need to get out of the cycle of poverty. Thus a person can make vocational choices for altruistic motives.

This is especially true with choosing celibacy, since a person does not choose it because he or she finds it enjoyable or sensually fulfilling, but because it will give that person the opportunity to do more for others with his or her life.

Margie: Don't celibate men and women feel sexually deprived? The idea of going a whole lifetime without any sexual release seems impossible and unbearable.

Father JP: Most celibate men and women have their sexual impulses under control and do not feel deprived. In a sense, it is like people who make a choice to remain virgins until marriage because they know it will express their love and commitment more completely, make their wedding night truly special, and cause their marriage together to be more fulfilling. They usually don't find that decision to be a burden, but something that frees them to really find and get to know their future spouse on a much deeper and more spiritual level. The same can be said of the person who chooses celibacy for the sake of God's kingdom.

I would even dare to say that a person who decides to wait until marriage for sexual relations actually enjoys his time dating better than the person giving in to his passion. In the same way, someone who says "yes" to a celibate vocation actually enjoys the good things in this life better while looking forward to an even better life in eternity.

Margie: Yet there is a kind of emotional support structure in marriage that helps a couple get through those rough times.

Father JP: The celibate man or woman may have emotional moments that reinforce their vocational decision. There may be special lights they receive while praying, the spiritual high they receive while making a retreat, the joy they receive having someone they have dealt with also say "yes" to God.

Nevertheless, the vocation to marriage and the vocation to living celibacy do not rely on whether we are affirmed by our emotions. The vocation depends on God's gift and our decision to correspond.

Margie: What about the other case of a person who feels called to marriage but doesn't think she can handle the sacrifice of children?

Father JP: Maybe that person doesn't have the talent or vocation for marriage if she really does not have the ability to handle children. However, one would have to see if this concern is because of selfishness or because of a call to another type of vocation.

Margie: Besides a few passing thoughts in high school, the topic of vocation never came up much until just a week or so ago. Will God give me any particular signs to help me tell whether I have a vocation to be a nun or to be a mother?

Father JP: Don't look for miraculous signs or voices telling you what to do. God doesn't normally work that way. He respects our freedom too much. He wants us to choose to give ourselves freely, whether in marriage or in celibacy.

Do you remember how the apostles reacted when Jesus told the people that a married couple could not lawfully divorce?

Margie: Something like, that if divorce is not a possible option, then it would better not to marry in the first place.

Father JP: You've got a good memory. Then Jesus goes on to say:

> *Not all men can receive this saying, but only those to whom it is given. For there are eunuchs who have been so from birth, and there are eunuchs who have been made eunuchs by men, and there are eunuchs who have made themselves eunuchs for the sake of the kingdom of heaven. He who is able to receive this, let him receive it.* (Matthew 19:11–12)

Some people are born with a congenital defect and unable to have sexual relations, but this is not a personal choice; it just happens. The same would be true for someone who became a eunuch by an act of violence. However, Our Lord spoke about those who would personally choose to remain celibate for the sake of His Kingdom. Yet, this is a gift, but not a gift for everybody; God "only" gives it to those whom he chooses, "to whom it is given."

God wants us to freely choose to respond to this gift (whatever the vocation, to marriage or to virginity and celibacy): "He who is able to receive this, let him receive it" (Matthew 19:12). So God will not give us such an overwhelmingly clear sign that we have no other choice but to say "yes."

Margie: How do we know what gift God has chosen to give us? That's a fair question to ask, isn't it?

Father JP: Certainly it is. Besides looking at the talents and gifts that God has given us, we may feel a strong attraction toward a particular vocation while experiencing a certain fear of following that path. All decisions involve risk. Because one's vocation is a life-orienting decision, the risk appears greater. Fear comes when one realizes the possible sacrifice that this call may entail. Perhaps there are uncertainties as well, such as, "What if it doesn't work out?" God never forces us to follow Him; our correspondence to grace is completely free, which can be quite a scary thing.

The Gospel recalls the incident of someone saying "no" to his vocation. A young man approached Our Lord to ask Him, "What must I do to have eternal life?" After going through the Ten Commandments with the young man, Our Lord said: "If you would be perfect, go, sell what you possess and give to the poor, and you will have treasure in heaven; and come, follow me." But the young man chose his possessions instead of following Christ, and because of that he was filled with great sadness (Matthew 19:16–22).

God gives us the gift of vocation to make us happy. Our happiness depends on our generosity. The real sign that this calling is the right one is the great sense of joy and peace that arises when one says "yes" to it. If this decision responds to an authentic call, it dispels our sadness, loneliness, and anxiety while giving our existence a sense of spiritual fullness and meaning.

Margie: When Sam and I talked about children and how we would raise them, I felt real joy about the possibility of marrying him. Then a real fear came over me: what if he really isn't the man for me? His not being Catholic is another real concern for me, yet he is so good in so many ways.

Father JP: Is this why you brought up the idea of having a possible vocation to the religious life? Is it a way to avoid the question of marrying Sam?

Margie: I don't know, Father JP. It may have been.

Father JP: I would encourage you to pray more about this. Until you say "yes" and experience the joy of giving yourself for life, that fear and uncertainty will remain. If we are open, discovering and living out our vocation is a great adventure. Ask God to give you light to see His will, "Lord, help me to see" (Luke 18:41). Ask our Blessed Mother to help you say "yes" to God's will with the same generosity that she did. Tell her that you want to give everything to God in that choice, whichever one you make. And listen to what the angel Gabriel said to Mary, "Do not be afraid" (Luke 1:30). Do not be afraid to make the choice to please God in everything rather than to have an easier life, for "He who loves his life loses it, and he who hates his life in this world will keep it for eternal life" (John 12:25).

Marriage depends on the agreement of three wills: the man's, the woman's, and God's. There is a mutual discernment going on: you have to discern whether Sam is right for you and Sam has to discern whether you are right for him. If you really love him, you will respect his freedom and be ready to leave him if you or he discerns that you are not meant for each other.

Pray that God may also resolve your concern over the disparity between your religious beliefs and Sam's. This is an important issue that will affect your children's happiness as well as your own.

Margie: Father JP, thank you. I do appreciate all that you have done for Sam and me. I'm sure that Sam does too.

Father JP: Well, the best way to thank me is to keep up the struggle. I'll be praying for you both.

221

Postscript

Margie and Sam continued their relationship for some time. . . .

You may realize that Margie and Sam are fictitious characters, although not entirely so. They represent the state of mind of many young people in search of authentic love and meaning in their relationships. The dialogue is real. It is a compilation of actual conversations, queries, and comments from many individuals.

However, many couples just like Margie and Sam — friends, neighbors, or acquaintances — would be happy to share their story with you. Perhaps they are at a different stage in their journey. The reader is encouraged to share with them what he or she has learned from Margie, Sam, and Father JP; then they may tell you the rest of their story.

Acknowledgments

This book is the fruit of many conversations: with high school and college students, young working men and women; with dating couples and those preparing for marriage, as well as with ones experiencing marital and family difficulties. Most of these conversations were one-on-one, but occasionally with couples. I am indebted to them all.

Although the idea for a book had been in my head for some time, the encouragement of Carlos and Mike was essential to get this started. Jesús, Patrick, and my sister Mary Kay were encouraging reviewers of the first very rough draft. Mary Kay and Alan did substantial work to put it in more readable form. I want to thank Jim and Maureen, Ralph and Bridget, Joe and Lorelei, Anthony, Alex, Chris, Fernando, Phil, Javier, Matt, and Raphael for their helpful suggestions, and Annie for her prayers.

I want to thank Joe and Chris for their ideas and artwork in illustrating this book.

The true inspiration for this book is Saint Josemaría Escrivá, the founder of Opus Dei, who always considered Christian purity and human sexuality as a positive affirmation of human love and love for God. Pope John Paul II's Christian personalism was key in developing my approach and ways of expressing the Christian teaching contained in this work.

Notes

1. Josemaría Escrivá, *Friends of God* (Princeton, N.J.: Scepter, 1981), 277, n. 177.

2. Alvaro del Portillo, *Cartas de Familia,* vol. 1 (Rome: Collegium Romanum Sanctae Crucis, 1989), 409, n. 380.

3. Cf. Servais Pinckaers, O.P., *The Sources of Christian Ethics* (Washington, D.C.: Catholic University of America Press, 1995), 438–39; George Weigel, *Witness to Hope: The Biography of Pope John Paul II* (New York: HarperCollins, 1999), 140.

4. Cf. George Weigel, *Witness to Hope,* 127.

5. Pope John Paul II, *Familiaris Consortio — The Role of the Christian Family in the Modern World* (Boston: Pauline Books and Media, 1981), 23, n. 11.

6. Pope John Paul II, *Mulieris Dignitatem — On the Dignity and Vocation of Women* (Boston: Pauline Books and Media, 1988), 88–90, n. 26. Cf. *Familiaris Consortio,* 86, n. 57.

7. John and Sheila K. Kippley, *The Art of Natural Family Planning,* 4th ed. (Cincinnati: Couple to Couple League, 1996), 245; Elóbieta Wójcik, "Natural Regulation of Conception and Contraception," in *Why Humanae Vitae Was Right: A Reader,* ed. Janet E. Smith (San Francisco: Ignatius Press, 1993), 431; Janet E. Smith, *Humanae Vitae: A Generation Later* (Washington, D.C.: Catholic University of America Press, 1991), 127.

8. Robert T. Michael, "Why did the U.S. Divorce Rate Double within a Decade?" in *Research in Population Economics,* vol. 6, ed. T. Paul Schultz (Greenwich, Conn.: JAI Press, 1988): 361–99.

9. Cf. Thomas W. Hilgers, M.D., and Joseph B. Stanford, M.D., M.S.P.H., "Creighton Model NaProEducation Technology for Avoiding Pregnancy: Use Effectiveness," in *Journal of Reproductive Medicine* 43 (St. Louis: June 1998): 495–502.

10. Charles Provan, *The Bible and Birth Control* (Monongahela, Pa.: Zimmer Printing, June 1989). John F. Kippley, M.D., *Birth Control and Christian Discipleship* (Cincinnati: Couple to Couple League, September 1993).

11. See Pope John Paul II, *Evangelium Vitae — On the Value and Inviolability of Human Life* (Vatican City: Libreria Editrice Vaticana, 1995), 18–21, nn. 13–14.

12. Mary Beth Bonacci, *Real Love: Mary Beth Bonacci Answers Your Questions on Dating, Marriage and the Real Meaning of Sex* (San Francisco: Ignatius Press, 1996), 73–75.

13. Ronald J. May, Ph.D., "The Challenge of Raising Emotionally Healthy Boys," in *Wisconsin Medical Journal* 101, n. 4 (May 2002): 43. Victor B. Cline, Ph.D., "Pornography's Effects on Adults and Children," monograph, Morality in the Media (New York, 2002).

14. Warren Clark, "Religious Observance: Marriage and Family," in *Canadian Social Trends* (Ottawa: Statistics Canada, Autumn 1998): 5. V. R. A. Call and T. B. Heaton, "Religious Influence on Marital Stability," *Journal for the Scientific Study of Religion* 36, n. 3 (1997): 382–92. Paul A. Nakonezny, Robert D. Schull, and Joseph Lee Rodgers, "The Effect of No-Fault Divorce Law on the Divorce Rate Across the 50 States and Its Relation to Income, Education and Religiosity," *Journal of Marriage and the Family* 57 (May 1995): 477–88.

15. E. Caparros, M. Thériault, and J. Thorn, eds., *Code of Canon Law Annotated* (Montréal: Wilson & Lafleur Limitée, 1993), 712–13, can. 1125.

16. In 1988, a group of scientists specializing in breast-feeding issued a statement called "The Bellagio Consensus." According to these scientists, "There is abundant evidence to show that a birth interval of two or more years significantly enhances infant survival and reduces maternal morbidity, particularly in less developed countries. Demographic data indicate that in many developing countries, the protection provided by breast-feeding alone is greater than that given by all other reversible means of family planning combined, and that breast-feeding makes a considerable contribution to securing a two year birth interval." Quoted in John and Sheila K. Kippley, *The Art of Natural Family Planning*, 339.

17. Marilyn M. Shannon, *Fertility, Cycles and Nutrition* (Cincinnati: Couple to Couple League, 1992); John and Sheila K. Kippley, *The Art of Natural Family Planning*, 333–54. Cf. Sheila K. Kippley, *Breastfeeding and Natural Child Spacing: How Ecological Breastfeeding Spaces Babies* (Cincinnati: Couple to Couple League, 1999).

18. Tertullian, *Ad Uxorem*, book 2, ch. 8, nn. 6–8, as quoted in Pope John Paul II, *Familiaris Consortio — The Role of the Christian Family in the Modern World*, 25, n. 13.

19. Elizabeth Moberly, Ph.D, *Psychogenesis: The Early Development of Gender Identity* (London: Routledge and Kegan Paul, Ltd., 1983), 9–16; Joseph Nicolosi, *Reparative Therapy of Male Homosexuality*

226

(Northvale, N.J.: Jason Aronson, 1997), 43–54; John F. Havery, O.S.F.S., *The Homosexual Person: New Thinking in Pastoral Care* (San Francisco: Ignatius Press, 1987), 37–48; Dale O'Leary "What Is Wrong With Same-Sex Marriage?" in *Catholic Exchange,* March 24, 2003 (Encinitas, Calif.).

20. John Gray, Ph.D., *Men are from Mars, Women are from Venus* (New York: HarperCollins, 1992).

21. Deborah Tannen, Ph.D., *You Just Don't Understand: Women and Men in Conversation* (New York: Ballantine Books, 1990).

22. Gary Smalley, *For Better or For Best: Understand Your Man* (New York: HarperPaperbacks, 1988) and *If Only He Knew: Joy that Lasts* (New York: HarperPaperbacks, 1988).

23. Pope John Paul II, *Mulieris Dignitatem — On the Dignity and Vocation of Women,* 66, n. 18.

24. Cf. Larry L. Bumpass, James A. Sweet, and Andrew Cherlin, "The Role of Cohabitation in Declining Rates of Marriage," *Journal of Marriage and the Family* 53 (November 1991): 913–27. Cf. Alfred DeMaris and K. Vaninadha Rao, "Premarital Cohabitation and Subsequent Marital Stability in the United States: A Reassessment," *Journal of Marriage and the Family* 54 (February 1992): 178.

25. Cf. Pope Paul VI, *Humane Vitae* (Boston: Pauline Books and Media, 1968), 4, n. 8, and Pope John Paul II, *Familiaris Consortio — The Role of the Christian Family in the Modern World,* 24–27, nn. 12 and 13.

For Further Reading

Javier Abad and Eugenio Fenoy, *Marriage: A Path to Sanctity* (Manila: Sinag-Tala, 1988). Starts with a Christian view of marriage and develops such topics as courtship and sexuality, chastity within marriage, children, and how to sanctify marriage.

Mary Beth Bonacci, *Real Love: Mary Beth Bonacci Answers Your Questions on Dating, Marriage and the Real Meaning of Sex* (San Francisco: Ignatius Press, 1996). This book consists of series of questions and answers that arose in the author's popular talks to high school students regarding human love, sexuality, and relationships. Very pragmatic in her answers.

Catechism of the Catholic Church (Washington, D.C.: United States Catholic Conference, 1994). The official Catholic teaching on topics of: vocation of laity and to religious life (nos. 897–945); marriage and virginity (nos. 1601–1666); chastity and sexuality (nos. 2331–2400; 2514–2533).

Jason Evert, *Pure Love* (San Diego: Catholic Answers, 1999). A concise and easy-to-read booklet, *Pure Love* covers all the major bases with answers to tough questions like: Is sex bad? Isn't everyone else doing it? Am I being good as long as I don't have sex?

———. *If You Really Loved Me: 101 Questions on Dating, Relationships, and Sexual Purity* (Ann Arbor, Mich.: Charis, Servant Publications, 2003). An expansion on *Pure Love,* delving into all kinds of dating/relationship questions. Helpful in avoiding many common and often painful mistakes people make in relationships.

Pope John Paul II (Karol Wojtyla), *Love and Responsibility* (San Francisco: Ignatius Press, 1993). Written while John Paul II was bishop of Krakow. A very deep exposition of human sexuality.

———. *Theology of the Body: Human Love in the Divine Plan* (Boston: Pauline Books & Media, 1997). A series of short reflections on Scripture regarding the nature of shame, modesty, purity, and the language of the body.

——. *The Meaning of Vocation: in the Words of John Paul II* (Princeton, N.J.: Scepter Publishers, 1997). An excellent resource on how God has a special plan or call for each individual, on the process of discerning that vocation, and on finding happiness in saying Yes to God.

John F. Kippley, M.D., *Birth Control and Christian Discipleship* (Cincinnati: Couple to Couple League, 1994). A great summary of the history of contraception and its effects on the physical well-being of individuals and the social well-being of society. Details the relationship between contraception and abortion.

Fulton J. Sheen, *Three to Get Married* (Princeton, N.J.: Scepter Publishers, 1997). A classic work on marriage and how God plays an essential role in marriage and in family life. Bishop Sheen is famous for being very clear and entertaining. With real-life stories of people whose lives were transformed by marriage and God.

Jerry Shepherd, *Teens and Relationships* (Sydney, Australia: Little Hills Press, 2001). Based on actual experience of teens in relationships, discusses how healthy human and Christian perspectives can enrich those relationships. Topics include friendship with peers and older people, and friendship with Christ.

Janet Smith, *Contraception: Why Not?* (Cincinnati, One More Soul). An audiotape of a talk that explains why the Catholic Church teaches that contraception is wrong as well as its detriments to physical health and relationships.

Christopher West, *Good News about Sex and Marriage: Answers to Your Honest Questions about Catholic Teaching* (Ann Arbor, Mich.: Charis, Servant Publications, 2000). In question-and-answer format, this book draws on the philosophical insights of John Paul II.

OF RELATED INTEREST

Donna Freitas and Jason King
SAVE THE DATE
A Spirituality of Dating, Love, Dinner, and the Divine

In this fun and lighthearted book by twenty-somethings Freitas and King, the authors present a positive view of dating, showing young people how dating can be a spiritual path that promotes maturity and growth. Topics include "I Love You" (Double-Click), When Friendship Isn't Enough, Making Dating Meaningful, Breaking Up Is Not Failure, and How Infatuation Differs from Love.

0-8245-2123-4, $18.95 paperback

Fran Ferder and John Heagle
TENDER FIRES
The Spiritual Promise of Sexuality

Who has not struggled with sexuality and religion? For decades, Sr. Fran Ferder, F.S.P.A, Ph.D., and Fr. John Heagle, M.A., J.C.L, have been listening to the stories of people's joys, sorrows, and dilemmas, as well as their efforts to integrate sexuality, faith, and church membership. In *Tender Fires,* Ferder and Heagle delicately reveal how the power of the erotic extends not just to sex but to every corner of existence. They explain how joy can be experienced in sexuality when it is seen as part of a dance that takes place in all facets of life. In short, the authors offer readers a truly prophetic vision for a renewed understanding of sexuality in the church.

"Here is a book as generous in its wisdom as it is exact in its observation of the human struggle to make the many voices of sexuality sing in harmony."
— Eugene Kennedy, author of *The Unhealed Wound*

0-8245-1982-5, $16.95 paperback

crossroad

OF RELATED INTEREST

Evelyn Eaton Whitehead and James D. Whitehead
THE WISDOM OF THE BODY
Making Sense of Our Sexuality

In *The Wisdom of the Body,* the Whiteheads explore the Christian sense of sexuality, drawing on biblical and theological resources, psychological and social research, and the communal wisdom of Christian lives.

0-8245-1954-X, $19.95 paperback

Richard Gaillardetz
A DARING PROMISE
A Spirituality of Christian Marriage

Gaillardetz, a prominent theologian and popular speaker, teaches that marriage sets a couple on a spiritual journey that promises romance and intimacy but also involves moments of fear, loneliness, and regret. He invites couples to celebrate their romance, but also to recognize that moments of loneliness and emptiness are equally a part of the fabric of married life — and part of the Paschal Mystery to which every Christian is called.

0-8245-1935-3, $16.95 paperback

Please support your local bookstore,
or call 1-800-707-0670 for Customer Service.

For a free catalog, write us at

THE CROSSROAD PUBLISHING COMPANY
481 Eighth Avenue, Suite 1550
New York, NY 10001

Visit our website at
www.crossroadpublishing.com
All prices subject to change.

crossroad